The MIRACLE EFFECT

Four Steps to Living
Heaven on Earth Every Day

Sylvia Vowless, QSM

I AM Mastery Series – Book 1

BALBOA
PRESS
A DIVISION OF HAY HOUSE

Balboa Press books may be ordered through booksellers or by contacting:

Balboa Press
A Division of Hay House
1663 Liberty Drive
Bloomington, IN 47403
www.balboapress.com.au
1 (877) 407-4847

Print information available on the last page.

ISBN: 978-1-5043-0124-4 (sc)
ISBN: 978-1-5043-0125-1 (e)

Balboa Press rev. date: 03/04/2016

Contents

Praise for the effectiveness of The Miracle Effect:

My wee apartment sold last night for exactly what I asked for after my "power-full" Sunday spent with you soaking up the content of the "Miracle Effect" message and my concentrated practice since then. Note: Even just 2 days' serious practice made the difference!! No one can believe what I got for it, especially with my not very good real estate agent and building property manager: $50K above the recent sales in the building. Who am I to question this Miracle?!

Sharalon Sutherland, *RN, PGDipBus,*
RetirementVillage Manager

Thank you so very much again for the excellent Miracle Effect information – in just a day it's already made a big difference on a few health issues I had!

A week later she added, *Yes, I am walking better and better without the stick!*

S. Mayes, Retired Secretary

Just a note to say thank you for the fantastic Miracle Effect course. Huge changes for me, a great opening of my connection to my Higher Self, and a sensation that I can only describe as spiritual ecstasy, as waves of energy moved around my body. I've processed and released a lot of past life experiences that were holding me back, and I'm waiting for new positive experiences to arise from these changes.

Gary Kinsey, Dip.Electronic Engineering UK,
Safety Advisor

Applying Sylvia's Miracle Effect to my own life is a wonderful adventure. It makes positive things happen at the perfect time in the perfect way, for the perfect reasons and for the highest good of all concerned. It certainly keeps me absolutely delighted with so many positive outcomes. And there is more where this comes from!

Ann Russell, author of the *Little Truff*
animal and conservation series

I am most impressed with the calibre of the Miracle Effect and depth of knowledge. You are a great example of someone who is living a Divinely inspired life. You obviously walk your talk and have well and truly integrated into your life the spiritual principles that you teach.

Terence J. Downey, Business Owner,
Thai Massage Practitioner, Rebirther

And a sampling of comments I've received from participants in my classes:

The information is so well structured and presented. Loved learning about seed causes, the on/off switches, and then Mind CPR—love this excellent quick-to-use tool! The four Diamond Laws are a real eye opener, helping me see subconscious beliefs that need to be erased.

Thank You, Thank You, Thank You – your work has changed my life!

Your Miracle Effect is truly inspirational with wonderfully transformational content.

Just wanted to say thanks. You have refined the information in such an understandable, use- friendly way, so it's very helpful and informative.

Dedication

*This book is dedicated
with awe and gratitude to its originator,
my I AM Higher Self,
my Divine Counterpart whose unfailing Power Source
makes living Heaven on Earth—and miracles—
so effortlessly and perfectly possible.*

*And to the memory of Dr Wayne Dyer
whose pioneering work shared this Higher Self concept
to the world, and upon whose shoulders I stand
to offer the next step of DIY empowerment.*

*Backstage following his last presentation, just three days
before he transitioned, it felt as though he was passing on
the torch with the big hug he gave me, the last he ever
gave to a member of the public.
Thank you, Wayne.*

Introduction

This is a book whose time has come. Everywhere I go, I hear people asking, *I believe miracles are possible, but **how** do I attract them and live a life of Heaven on Earth every day?* This evolutionary book is the much-needed answer.

The Miracle Effect has one goal: to help you with factual information and proven tools to super-charge your life and make miracles your daily habit. This guidebook is a goldmine of so many things you wish you'd always known, together with bullet-proof strategies to implement them. In it, you will learn the steps to open up previously unknown realms of breath-taking possibilities for yourself.

You will learn how to:

♥ *Turn your dreams into reality*, so you never have to settle for less.

♥ *Strengthen your spiritual "mind muscles,"* so you can utilize their enormous latent power every day to create and enjoy a life less ordinary.

♥ *Raise your consciousness to the next level*, or as high as you can go in the shortest time possible.

♥ *Restore your full Higher Self energy flow and activate* your dormant Divine abilities and potential.

♥ *Eradicate or transform hidden traps* that, if left active, will stop your progress and success dead in its tracks.

♥ *Enhance the flow of your life* through aligning your subconscious and conscious minds with your Higher Mind.

- ♥ *Live in harmony with the governing laws of life,* the Laws of Universal Principles, and apply them to your thoughts, feelings, words and actions for complete effectiveness.
- ♥ *Create the environment for ongoing miracles to occur* through amazing events and circumstances, support and connections, that fill you with awe and delight.

Be Realistic—Expect Miracles— Become a Miracle Magnet!

Since my first experience of consciously creating a miracle nearly a decade ago, I've developed the ability to dependably repeat this experience in different situations. Many of the miracles I've created have been life-changing. Many defy all known physical explanation. Had I not discovered the Miracle Effect and begun to take the steps to make it a reality in my life, instead of the perfect health I now enjoy, I would be in constant pain, unable to walk or stand and live a normal life. I'd also be struggling financially and severely limited in countless other ways.

Today, my life is full of wonder and miracles, a perfect expression of what Heaven on Earth looks like to me— miracles are like the icing on the cake. And in deep gratitude for my extraordinary life, it's my joy to share with you the unique, four-step methodology I've developed and taught for creating a life like mine. The method I teach is based not upon my beliefs or on dogma, but upon ancient wisdom principles that I've distilled from more than four decades of study and research, blended with my understanding of relevant, modern science.

What you are about to learn is not all theory, however. Having been a teacher for nearly 60 years and counting, I've learned to translate profound concepts into easy-to-understand language and practical tools. I've taught the content of this guidebook countless times in seminars, helping me to hone my presentation and refine the techniques. I explain the principles in a simple and user-friendly way. Most importantly, I explain how you can apply them to every situation of your regular daily life just as I do, until miracle-making becomes a way of life, a habit you rely on as sure as brushing your teeth or taking a daily walk—like developing a miracle habit.

Having gained so much from my personal experience, I offer you this guidebook so you too can learn to live a life of effortless mastery and abundance – and miracles. The key to creating this kind of life is something I call the *I AM Mastery* effect, and this book is the first of a series about how to develop such higher spiritual power. As the late Dr. Wayne Dyer, an inspirational pioneer in this field, once said, "You'll be happy to know that the Universal Law that created miracles has not been repealed!"

What is a Miracle?

Any guidebook on how to live a miracle-filled life must first introduce exactly what is the often-times misunderstood definition of the word *miracle*. Coming from the Latin word meaning "to wonder at," the word *miracle* today describes a marvel, something that goes far beyond normal expectations. Miracles occur as events, synchronicities, unexpected happenings or connections that defy belief and often defy logic.

So what makes it possible to become a "miracle magnet" and attract such wonders on a regular basis into your everyday life? Miracles depend upon you raising your awareness to a level of consciousness above the normal human perception of limitations and uncertainty. You create a mental and spiritual environment of unlimited possibilities, free of any trace of doubt. The frequency of miracles in your life depends upon how well you are able to maintain this, and the steps for developing that ability follow in this book.

My deeper understanding of miracles comes from a seven-year study I began in 1985 of *A Course in Miracles (ACIM)*, a book channeled by a Columbia University professor who was encouraged by a colleague to write down what she heard inside. This beautiful book helps you to know yourself on a deep, spiritually psychological level. Today, exactly 30 years later, I was prompted to dust off my copy of *ACIM* and open its well-thumbed pages to look up what it says about the meaning and principles of miracles.

I'm awestruck. Even though I hadn't consciously remembered the list of 50 fundamental principles for miracle creation listed in *ACIM*, I find among them the foundation for how I now live a miracle-filled life and what makes my techniques work successfully.

One truth immediately caught my eye: *You are a miracle who is capable of creating in the likeness of your Creator, and everything else is your own nightmare.* Another principle states that miracles can become habits, adding that they are everyone's right, and for us as divinely-created beings, they are natural. But first we are cautioned to clear our mind of illusions in order to practice this natural right. You are about to understand this truth, and most importantly, how to permanently rid your thinking of illusions and all else that might hold you back or get in your way.

Think of this: What if you could install your own personal inner mentoring program to guide and support you to create miracles in your life? What if you could learn to magnetize miracles as a habit, adding a diamond-like sparkle to transform your experience of life even more? All this user-friendly array of empowering knowledge is now at your finger-tips in this guidebook.

As you start using my step-by-step processes found nowhere else, you will experience your ordinary, treadmill life transforming into a purposeful and miraculous adventure. You will feel relief and peace as old frustrations and struggles ebb away, giving you a deep sense of empowerment to make undreamed-of possibilities become your everyday reality.

About This Guidebook

What you're about to read really works. My message is simple: by honouring your divinity and learning to live fearlessly and confidently from your I AM Higher Self, you can learn to manifest your deepest desires with ease and certainty.

I'm a living testament to that fact, having proved these techniques and methods over and over again in my personal life. I've also seen countless others proving it for themselves as they too learn and apply what is necessary to become a miracle magnet, sometimes with almost immediate results. This is why I can promise it will work for you. All you have to do is take the steps I lay out clearly for you to follow, steps that will transform you into the manifestation master you were designed to be—a *Miracle Me*.

The contents of this guidebook are divided into four main parts that are the major steps of my methodology. Together, these steps (more like giant strides!) guide you through the understandings and their applications you need to break the chains of limitation and become free to be all you were created to be. Each step is made up of numerous smaller steps essential to your progress and success. Together they build on one another to provide a firm foundation upon which you can confidently progress, proving for yourself through practice that the tools and techniques are credible and dependable.

Step One, **Know Who You Really Are,** explores the real you, not simply the personality you are known by, but who you really are, an expression of divinity. The premise and success of becoming a miracle magnet rests upon you fully understanding and embracing this profound truth— and then living it. Your physical human self rests upon the foundational sciences of Vibration and Mind and the Universal Laws of Thought, so an outline of these concludes this step. Without understanding these basic laws, you risk staying stuck in a *Groundhog Day* kind of existence, repeating the same events in a loop of unconscious choices and actions, day after day.

Step Two, **Breakthrough Keys on Your Path to Success,** explains how to identify what is stopping your success, those hidden causes that act like on/off switches regulating your progress. Many of these blocks are due to ignorance of the inescapable Universal Laws that govern us all, whether they are known or not. You'll learn about the five Breakthrough Keys to clear those factors that prevent or severely limit any kind of life improvement you desire.

Step Three, **How to Unlock the Secrets of Your Success,** is all about the "how-to," teaching you to use my four unique Master Secrets and their empowering applications essential for your evolution as a miracle magnet.

It includes many examples that provide rock-solid proof that these manifestation techniques always work.

***Step Four*, Design Your Life to Live Heaven on Earth,** covers the *designing*, *daring*, and *doing* aspect of miracle mastery. In this step, you learn about my Perfect Diamond of Life technique, what I've found to be a "gem beyond price" because it encompasses so well everything you may desire or require for an amazing life. Expressed graphically, the Perfect Diamond supports you to apply all the priceless knowledge you will by then have acquired in highly practical and specifically targeted ways for designing your life of Heaven on Earth.

Although you will probably return to read this book again and again, by the end of it you will be equipped to step into your own latent divine power and magnificence as a Miracle Me, a person able to achieve unstoppable and repeatable success. This is the promise of cultivating your life as a miracle effect, but then it's up to you to choose how to live your life.

Albert Einstein once said, "There are only two ways to live your life. One is as though nothing is a miracle. The other is as though everything is a miracle."

I've made my choice. Which do you choose?

Prologue

Something happened in the summer of 2006 that changed my life forever.

It seemed straightforward enough: Spend the day flying from Copenhagen to Montpellier, France, and then take a direct train east to Arles. A good night's sleep and I'd be fresh and ready for the seminar at 10 AM the next morning.

Departure time for my flight was 7:30 AM, giving me plenty of time to arrive at Montpellier and get my train at 2 PM. But then this became 8 AM, and after that, an 11 o'clock departure was posted.

Still possible to catch the train and arrive in Arles by dinner time, I thought.

Then an announcement came over the airport speaker system: *We regret to announce that estimated departure time for Montpellier is now 7:30 PM*. Oh dear, no public transport will be running after I get in at 10 tonight—*What to do?*

As I sat there trying to figure a way out of my dilemma, a potential solution struck me. For years, as a spiritually trained and practiced person, I accepted that my Higher Self was an unfailing source of divine power and miracles, but I'd never consciously put it to the test in any specific way. I decided that now was the perfect time to do that.

I spent the day in the airport in a meditative state, consciously communicating with my divine power source through speaking inwardly with my Divine Presence the Holy Spirit. I clearly stated my desire to somehow reach Arles in time and asked for help in creating the environment for a miracle to manifest. And it did.

I arrived in Arles at 1 AM, able to check into my hotel and still have time to get some sleep before showing up the next morning at the seminar on time feeling rested and refreshed. (My full story of how this happened is in the Appendix.)

The incredible sequence of events that solved what seemed to be an impossible situation simply happened without much effort on my part. The resulting miracle—the first of many—set me off on my nine-year quest to discover what lay behind such out-of-the-ordinary occurrences, and how I could make them more of a habit in my life.

I'm a pragmatist at heart. Things have to make sense to me. Even back then, I somehow knew that this exciting result did not have to be a one-off. There had to be underlying principles that, if understood, would make it possible not only to repeat other miraculous outcomes but do so quickly.

The I AM Mastery foundation is the answer, which, together with my *Miracle Effect* techniques, add an undreamed of dimension to my life.

My Story

My life hasn't always been so miraculous and wonder-filled. Since my humble beginnings, I've overcome many obstacles, many fears and limiting beliefs along the way to make my dreams a reality.

Born in London just before WWII broke out, I spent my first seven years under the black cloud of wartime fear and deprivation, moving continually with my mother to escape the relentless bombing of my country by Nazi Germany. The world I knew was one of uncertainty and fear with death and destruction raining down from the skies day and night. Huddled night after night in a tiny cupboard under the stairs that served as our home air raid shelter, lit by a single candle, we accepted this regular situation as "normal." Even today I get the shivers when I hear the sound of a siren in a movie.

Listening to the whistle of falling bombs, waiting the few heart-thumping seconds of silence before they hit the ground and exploded, but never knowing how close they would be, was a common experience. No-one ever knew if we'd be wiped out by the next bomb, or whether we'd see our loved ones, particularly dads, ever again. Food was scarce, and we were often hungry for something more than just another slice of bread and jam.

This early experience left me with a belief that the world is not a safe place, that life is difficult and a struggle, and there's never enough to go round. Fortunately, I was blessed with an amazing mother who, as a born optimist, did her best to shield me from an overload of negative effects. Even so, she recalled that during one relentless air-raid filled night, I asked her why her teeth were chattering. I chose my parents well.

In 1950, my family emigrated to New Zealand, my true "soul's home," but the familiar pattern of life-is-hard-and-uncertain continued. Money was extremely scarce because after paying the boat passage for all of us, my parents had only two thousand pounds with which to start a new life. I carried this belief that life is a struggle for many, many years. Bringing up my son alone without support lent further proof to this unconscious program.

Fast forward to 1968 when my questioning about the meaning of life began to move me beyond my conventional upbringing and religion-based background. After my marriage broke up in 1977, I immersed myself in the ancient teachings that Alduous Huxley called the *Perennial Wisdom*. I began to realize that life is what we make it, although I was extremely sceptical of the manifestation mastery concept at first, particularly when applied to money. But I decided to put my new-found knowledge to the test in several ways and soon found that yes, it is possible, and spectacularly so.

In the 1980s, my life's journey took a different turn. My knowledge and understandings suddenly started expanding rapidly as I learned how to meditate deeply every day. This enabled me to make direct contact with my Higher Self mind and to hear the "still, small voice" within. Profound revelations began to download into my conscious mind, including those that showed how to practically apply ageless wisdom teachings. Life ceased to be a constant struggle as I began to develop my Self-empowerment.

I was inspired to begin sharing some of this by creating a community-based programme I called *Master your Life*. The programme proved very popular, but because of the PC attitudes prevalent in those days, my classes had to appear as a secular, not spiritual or religious offering. I kept quiet about the fact that what I was teaching actually originated in meditation and was delivered to me as direct downloads.

Today things are quite different, and I not only reveal my Higher Self source of knowledge, but I help others to access their own. Learning how to do this, I've come to realize, is the most important step of spiritual progress each of us can take.

In 1990, a suggestion from my inner guidance had me sell up everything I owned—house, car, furniture, and other possessions, so all that was left were three boxes of personal items stored in my parents' garage. The suggestion was for me to buy a one-way ticket back to England where I would learn to implicitly trust my inner voice, and await further guidance. Being in my early 50s, this was quite a scary idea, but by then I was serious that my spiritual advancement was all that mattered. With a brave, big gulp, I took a leap of faith and set out on a life-changing adventure.

The year-long experience of having no home base brought up all sorts of fears around security and trust that had been lurking in my subconscious mind since early childhood. Once I managed to let go of being in control however, amazing things started happening. As soon as I learned how to listen to the perfect and infallible guidance from the Divine Presence within me—and act upon it—my life shifted into a higher gear.

After my return home to New Zealand, I started sharing the spiritual understandings I had gained and the practical tools I had developed during my sojourn in England, in the form of sacred Soul Path trainings and initiations which continue to this day.

For these past 30 years, my life and service as guided by my Higher Self has slowly blossomed into the most fulfilling experience imaginable, and I wouldn't have wanted to miss a minute of it—including the numerous challenges as well as the incredible highs. The difference is that now not only do I fully understand how I create life's obstacles but also how to see the gifts and lessons in those challenges, and so handle them gracefully. My "soul service" to date has taken me seven times around the world, speaking at international spiritual conferences, teaching in many countries and meeting extraordinary people and colleagues. I AM so blessed and deeply grateful.

It has taken years of conscious, deliberate work, trial and error, to erase and replace the powerful conditionings and beliefs of my formative years, but the result has been well worth the effort. Now 70 years later, I am done with struggling and striving. I am free of fear, including fear of lack, because I now have 100 percent trust in my I AM Higher Self.

Sylvia Vowless, QSM

Birth of This Book

After a divine intervention miracle saved me from undergoing an unnecessary knee surgery earlier this year (2015), I settled back to my usual contemplation and meditation routine.

Up until that time, all plans had been put on hold, as I had been warned I wouldn't be able to do much during the recovery months. My diary for the first half of the year was blank, something that had never happened before, so I asked my Higher Self to reveal my next most perfect step in fulfilling my soul's purpose. Soon my Higher Self inspired me with the idea of creating a one-day workshop that I called Miracle Me, an event that has since proved outstanding in its life-changing effects at every presentation.

The divine intervention miracle of my near-surgery experience had brought to my attention the fact that here was another example of how miracles can occur. Looking back, I realized that I'd experienced miracles of the other three kinds (these are explained in Chapter 12), particularly during the previous ten years. Now my Higher Self was prompting me to share my miracle-working concepts and practical tools with others.

As I worked to put the workshop together, I realised three things: 1) all my previous years' study and practice provided the foundation for what I could now understand and do; 2) I'd unconsciously been testing a Miracle Effect manifestation mastery theory in various situations and developing my own techniques to repeat the exciting results, as and when I wished; and, 3) this process was taking far longer than I'd expected!

I started to think: *Why is it taking me so long to put together just a one day workshop when I'm quite used to creating annual weekend and longer events quite effortlessly?* I found myself going back again and again to restructure the sequence of teachings, adding or subtracting topics, developing some parts more than usual, and so on. Eventually it dawned on me. What I was doing was not just designing the program for the workshop—it was the format for a new book.

Two years earlier, I'd drafted a book based purely on the Universal Laws, deliberately omitting any mention or reference to the spiritual foundation of my work. But it hadn't felt right, and so I put the manuscript on the shelf and left it. I now realized that I would have to start from scratch and write from a totally different angle—one in which I was true to myself by including the higher spiritual source of the book's content.

I'd thought my earlier manuscript would reach more people by being overtly non-spiritual. But in 2015, my Higher Self guided me to attend a seminar led by the late Dr. Wayne Dyer who talked about how he lived and wrote from awareness of his personal I AM or Higher Self foundation. He explained this as a dimension of our being that transcends limitations of the physical world and empowers us to be all we can be. This is exactly the premise of my life, too.

The Miracle Effect is about the next big step of how to put Wayne Dyer's message into action. Hearing him speak about this for the entire weekend confirmed for me that people worldwide are now ready for the I AM-based knowledge and understanding. At times, I felt Wayne's spirit hovering over this book – from the first moment we met our shared philosophy and experiences created a connection.

And so *The Miracle Effect* was birthed. I trust that coming from its perfect and complete form in the non-material world known as the Quantum Field, the wisdom has been scribed well enough herein to fulfil its purpose now in the physical realm. Your own experience, dear reader, will be the proof of how well what is between these pages works to enhance and uplift your life to a Heaven on Earth level.

I'd love to hear your success stories. I can be reached through my website at: www.sylviavowless.com

STEP I:
Know Who You Really Are

CHAPTER 1

The Most Important Moment in Your Life

For when you know yourself, your sense of limited identity vanishes, and you know that you and your God-Self are one and the same.

Ibn 'Arabi, 12th Century Sufi Mystic

What could possibly transcend the moments you consider the greatest in your life—the birth of a child, falling in love for the first time, achieving a treasured goal or outstanding success—and be more important than anything else?

The most important moment in your whole life is when you realize with a mind-opening flash of recognition that the purely physical human "you" is only a pale shadow of who you truly are. In such a moment, you suddenly go beyond intellectual knowing, beyond mere lip-service, to accepting and embracing the fact that you are a Divine Being in physical expression. You see your small, limited life, and it suddenly dawns on you to ask yourself the now-obvious question, *Why on earth am I still struggling?*

This defining, life-changing moment leads to the profound realization that you can choose to demonstrate your divinity and its boundless potential in your everyday life. You decide then and there to stop living in a continual state of striving, fear, lack and unpleasant limitation. Instead, you shift your consciousness to a higher level and take the first steps towards expressing your true magnificence.

From that moment, you begin seeking ways to adopt the God-Habit of allowing the expression of your Higher Self perfection as your everyday mode of living. You move into a state of knowingness of your true potential: one who, as Deepak Chopra wisely noted, doesn't try to solve the mystery of life but instead lives it.

Reading this book will give you the much-needed know-how to do that. You are about to take your first step on the way to embodying your divinity.

Know Your Real Self

Think of your amazing body that is made up of over 50 trillion cells designed to work together as a harmonious community. Think of your incredible brain and its continual neural activity. The average human brain has about 100 billion neurons, and each one can be connected to up to a thousand trillion synaptic connections. No wonder it's said that our brains are like the greatest bio-computer ever created.

Think of this: in the course of a day you have 30 to 50 thousand thoughts flitting through your mind—another miracle. And not forgetting the vast range of human emotions you have to choose from, as well as your individual personality that makes you unique. All are miracles of expression. You are indeed a miracle of creation.

But wait—there's so much more! Do all the above make up the *real* you? Is there something even greater, even more miraculous about each one of us?

The answer is *yes*. What you know as your human identity is not your essence, not your real self, not the real you. It's only a limited physical expression of who you truly are, which is a Divine Being with limitless possibilities

4

incarnate. The most perfect expression of your Divine Being while in human form is what I'm calling your potential *Miracle Me*.

You Are Divine

Your Divine Being is not just a lofty title or grandiose idea with only a spiritual application. It is in fact the real you, and a way of being and living from your highest potential. This is the very first principle to understand and embrace if you wish to be all you can be, both human and spiritual—who you are meant to be. Reclaiming your inherent divine power gives you the life you were destined to live.

This Divine Being is known by many names—Higher Self, I AM or I AM Presence, God-Self, Overself, Divine Self, Impersonal Self, fifth-dimensional Body of Light, Sacred Self, Divine Counterpart, to name a few. You can choose whichever name you prefer. (Notice I use upper case letters for divine names to differentiate between them and the lower, personality self.)

No matter what name you use, they all relate to your personal divine source of power. That source has always been in existence, even long before you decided to experience living in "schoolhouse earth." That source is the eternal, immortal aspect of every person that fortunately remains unaffected by anything you choose to do in any lifetime on earth. *This is the truth of who you really are.* And its eternal nature is summed up in Jesus' saying: "Before Abraham was, I AM." (John 8:58)

Some people, however, prefer to use a more generic, less personal term for their higher power source, such as the Universe, Spirit, the Force, Infinite Intelligence, or simply God. The reason I prefer a more specific expression is that it feels closer and more accessible. I see my Higher Self as my Divine Counterpart, an aspect of myself just waiting for me to access and use for the greatest good of myself and others as I play out my current role as "Sylvia."

Once you learn to identify with your real Self rather than identifying with your human self, then nothing is impossible. You discover that your unfailing, divine Self is always present and available, closer than breathing. It longs for you to become acquainted with It and allow Its gifts to manifest as any and every thing you could possibly require and desire, including miracles.

This is your life assignment as a Divine Being, to live your life as an example that inspires others. Then you will enhance many people's lives as well as your own.

I AM Light

In the Western spiritual tradition, the Divine Mind of the Godhead is known as *I AM that I AM,* an infinite consciousness or intelligence that animates and sustains all life. There's no place this intelligence is not, and yet it can't be known by us directly.

This Infinite Consciousness began creation using pure Superluminal or Cosmic Light, a light that is limitless. Cosmic Light is an emanation of Divine Love, so I often refer to it as Love-Light. In this sense, Love-Light is the highest possible vibration that condenses into form. All of creation is therefore condensed light, a Love-Light energy that is also within everyone and keeps us all alive.

From the *I AM that I AM* Godhead came your individual expression known as your I AM Presence, meaning that you are always connected to your divine origin. Your personal I AM Presence carries the name of the Godhead and is your blueprint, a fifth-dimensional body of condensed Divine Love-Light. Your I AM Presence is also directly connected to what is called the *quantum field*, the *source field*, or *zero point field* (ZPF), an expression of the Infinite Consciousness that contains all potentialities and information.

Your I AM emanated a reflection or lower counterpart of Itself, that you know as a soul. This is necessary so you can experience what it is like to live in this dense, third dimension of life on earth. Think of your soul as a consciousness body that protects and houses the divine spark of your I AM God-Self, a tiny flickering flame of pure Divine Love-Light that will eventually expand until, with your conscious effort, it floods and transforms your whole being.

Of course, to travel the earth plane the soul needs a vehicle, a physical body made up of bio-chemicals and powered by subatomic photons. Both rely on solar light to function in the material realm yet are animated by the divine Cosmic Light.

The Divine Spark within your soul gives you direct access to limitless higher power, and like a candle flame it never diminishes, no matter how much you use it to light up your life. In fact, the more you use it to bring Love-Light into expression in this physical realm, the more the flame expands, making even greater Divine Power available to you.

As the original I AM master, Jesus gave us many clues in his most powerful statements that mostly began with I AM. He also said that by himself, he could do nothing. This is your divine birthright too, the foundation of your Miracle Me Self.

Your Higher Self lineage enables you to utilize higher dimensional solutions for earth-bound problems. Einstein wisely commented that we can't fix a problem on the same level where it was created. Only a higher level solution can be truly successful. Just how right Einstein was you are about to see, as you journey with me through *The Miracle Effect.*

The fact that you are even reading this book tells you that these understandings are what you personally signed up for in your current life. The grave is not your goal—living as a divine Miracle Me is your purpose.

Are you ready right now to live your glorious mission to its fullest extent and be a shining example to inspire others? Whatever you do, don't ever be afraid to blossom and unfold your inner Light. Remind yourself often: *I AM Light.*

CHAPTER 2

I AM Communication

You may be wondering, *I understand who I am now, but how can I consciously connect with my real Self?* The answer is the subject of this chapter.

The Holy Spirit

You have a divine presence within called the Holy Spirit that serves as the connecting link with your I AM Higher Self. Holy Spirit is the communicator, or *still, small voice within* that acts like a phone line to your Higher Self. *A Course in Miracles* states that the Holy Spirit within is the mechanism through which miracles are created, and is the highest spiritual communication device we have.

Once you've learned to work with this wonderful gift, you find it is the means for you to receive Higher Mind information, knowledge, inspiration and guidance whenever you require it.

So how does the Holy Spirit work?

To help you understand the interconnection between Higher Self and your human experience, I've created a diagram that clearly shows the "line of higher communication," while summarizing the main meanings of each level.

Line of Higher Communication

This diagram below shows how you can choose to have your Higher Mind in charge as director of your life, and change ego self-will to Higher Self-will.

INFINITE DIVINE MIND
of the
I AM that I AM
illumines your
Higher Mind
of your
I AM Higher Self

The interconnecting link and inner voice
of your I AM Higher Self is the
Holy Spirit
which communicates with your
Soul,
then your
Subconscious Mind
and
Conscious Mind
that has the power of

Self-mastery - Choice - Universal Laws
and controls your
Emotional Body and Physical Body

Your Divine GPS System

As you can see from the Line of Higher Communication diagram, the Holy Spirit is also the connecting link between your Soul, subconscious and conscious minds, as well as your Higher Self. Although the Holy Spirit is called a *voice*, most people rarely have an auditory experience. Instead, the communication comes through an unmistakable sense of knowing, or an *Aha!* that suddenly provides the information or guidance being sought.

I often think of the Holy Spirit as my hotline to my Higher Self Mind. I see it as my own personal link acting like a higher GPS guidance system. It's there to help advise me when making important life choices or knowing how best to act, react or handle a given situation or challenge, so I can keep on the right track.

All we have to do is to ask for help. But therein lie some possible hiccups. The biggest one is forgetting that you cannot access divine guidance unless you are in the energies of love and trust that are necessary for connecting with the divine realm. The main use of Higher Self guidance is for life-changing or major decisions and definitely not for trivial things like what to wear today. The Holy Spirit is there to help support you become a Self-master.

Not knowing the best way to ask, or even what to ask, is another hiccup. If you'd like to learn clear guidelines for how to ask and have the best communication possible with Holy Spirit, my *Spiritual Wisdom* YouTube channel series will help you. In particular, the second and third mini-seminars deal specifically with this topic. Here are the links:

2/6 Tapping into your Soul Guidance: **https://www. youtube.com/watch?v=qN2fbj2VRr0**

Sylvia Vowless, QSM

3/6 Activating your Holy Spirit Hot-Line: **https://www.
youtube.com/watch?v=LHM6XEEbyy0**

Note: Keeping It Simple

Instead of having to say or write the full Higher Self-
Holy Spirit wording every time, I use a shortened version
for reference—HS. Since the two—Holy Spirit and Higher
Self—function inextricably as one, using the same initials
for both underscores their relationship and the fact that they
always work together. Going forward, I'll mainly use the HS
abbreviation for this partnership.

CHAPTER 3
Gifts of Your I AM Higher Self

Let's define more precisely what your I AM God-Self encompasses as an unfailing source of higher power, so its awesome gifts become real to you.

Spiritual MRI

We're all familiar with the detailed physical information an MRI scan reveals. I use a spiritual analogy for a different kind of MRI—*M*odern *R*elevant *I*nterpretation—as a way of translating ancient wisdom principles and teachings from sacred texts into concise contemporary descriptions. In particular, I use my MRI to explain exactly what the I AM Higher Self represents, and most importantly, what living from this exhilarating, freeing understanding looks like in everyday, three-dimensional terms. In modern colloquial terms, "to get a handle on it."

The way I've been given to express the gifts and relevance of our divine I AM Higher Self Counterpart is as an *-ism*, meaning a condition or system that makes this important foundational concept usable.

As an extension of the *I AM that I AM* Godhead, your individualized I AM Higher Self naturally has divine attributes. And they're yours for the asking. To summarize and remember the most important aspects, I received the inspired anagram of PEOPLISM. Using this arrangement of letters perfectly highlights the fact that these divine attributes apply to all people.

Every person has their own Higher Counterpart and therefore has access to its miraculous potential. The aim of the following anagram is to help you permanently imprint the huge scope of your latent possibilities in your memory and to embody its practical relevance into your consciousness. Have fun testing yourself until you can recall every one of the letter-meanings effortlessly, so they become real, working aspects in your life to use every day.

PEOPLISM

P - Power Source—and **Peace**. As already described, the Higher Self directly carries the unlimited Divine Love-Light of creation. This means it's the highest personal source of God Power you can in any moment easily tap into for doing, being or manifesting anything you can think of and desire. There are no limits, except in your thinking.

Once you fully embody this understanding, deep unshakeable inner peace automatically follows. Never again will you feel alone, powerless or limited.

E – Energy. Similarly, this is your eternal, unbounded energy source for both your mind and physical body, and for converting into whatever form you choose. Physics states that energy can never be lost, only transformed into some other form. As a conscious expression of your Higher Self incarnate, you have the ability to direct this energy in unlimited ways, as you'll be learning further on in this guidebook. **E** is also for **Excellence**. Excellence is an achievable and worthy goal, whereas absolute perfection as you'll read below, is unattainable in this world.

O – Origin/Outcome (or Destination). Your I AM is the original Divine Blueprint for your physical being that is also coded in your DNA as what Gregg Braden has termed the *God Code* (see Appendix). Each body you have used for your many life experiences on earth is an expression of this blueprint, perfectly adapted to suit your soul's purpose and lessons chosen for that incarnation.

Eventually when you've completed the need to keep reincarnating, your soul will have finished its job and will be able to re-unite with its origin, your Higher Self I AM. This is known as *ascension,* and it is the ultimate outcome or goal of each person's countless cycles of reincarnation—your destination. (My workshop, *Master Path of Soul Ascension,* gives ten key principles to help you identify the steps you and every person must take to reach your destination. Check my website for details, ominternational.nz)

P – Perfection and Beauty. In a world based upon polarity and duality, there can never be perfection in the purest, cosmic sense. But because the Divine Mind can only think thoughts of perfection and beauty, you as an expression of this are able to enjoy the highest levels possible in this physical realm, including miracles, when you allow your perfect Higher Self to work through you. Appreciation of beauty in every form gives you glimpses of perfection.

L – Limitlessness. I love the late Dr. Wayne Dyer's words: "There is one grand lie—that we are limited. The only limits we have are the limits we believe."

As soon as you realize this, you can begin to transcend your old limited mindset and way of life because you remember that the substance of all creation is Divine Love-Light, which must be limitless. As your Miracle Me Self emerges and your limited beliefs melt away, all manner of amazing possibilities previously unknown open up beyond the usual human perceptions. The strength to release all false sense of lack and deprivation becomes available to you, releasing your mind from the imprisonment of its third-dimensional shackles of illusions.

I – Intelligence, Illumination (or knowledge), **and Inspiration**. Tapping into your I AM Higher Mind source of extraordinary intelligence is exciting. It's as though a light shines into your awareness, and you suddenly find you have knowledge and understanding far beyond what was previously available. Great musicians, writers, and inventors throughout history have all attributed their genius to inspiration coming from a higher source.

But for everyday folk like us, it's still wonderful to be inspired with great ideas, solutions to problems, ways you can be a more effective instrument for service, and to create a heavenly life. Whenever you require power and strength to achieve something worthwhile—providing you remember to stay out of your own way by not relying on your little human self—you allow the Intelligence of your enormous, divine birthright to illuminate your life.

S – Substance, Strength and **Serenity**. Becoming a co-creator with your God-Self, you know without any doubt that you can direct with Higher Power and Strength the universal substance into whatever kind of life and form you choose, easily and perfectly. This knowing produces a profound sense of certainty and peace of mind that can be summed up as an inner serenity nothing can shake. In today's frenetic world this is a stupendous gift.

M – Manifestation, Mastery and **Miracles**. I enjoy seeing how many miracles I can allow to manifest on a regular basis. Big or small, they marvelously enhance everyday living. There are no limits as to how or in what way they can occur. Of course, the old ways of manifesting through mind power, countless affirmations every day, the Law of Attraction, and so on, are still valid for those who wish to do it that way. But by now, you are beginning to sense there is a higher way that transcends the need for time-consuming methods, if you choose to use it.

Developing the Miracle-Habit

Unleashing your I AM power takes manifestation mastery to the highest and most perfect expression possible. Once you've awakened to your latent abilities, life will never be the same, and you'll never want to go back to the old ways.

Keeping the knowing of who you truly are in the forefront of your mind quickly develops the God-Habit way of thinking, a state of mind that transcends third-dimensional limitations in every challenge or situation throughout each day. All you have to do is accept and develop this understanding in your thinking, feeling and doing.

I use the image of riding on a hovercraft, skimming above anything of the physical vibration that would limit me. The God-Habit is a blissful and effortless way to live, and it is the foundation for you in cultivating a miracle effect.

CHAPTER 4
Physically, You Are Vibration and Mind

Once you are determined to start manifesting your perfect life, the very first basic understanding you must acquire concerns the energetic mechanics of your physical, emotional and mental selves. This is summed up by the two foundational groups of laws concerning *vibration* and *mind*, and how well you stay in alignment with them in your daily living.

Energy and Your Thoughts

In science, it's known that all creation rests on the foundation of vibrational energy. Everything is made of energy, and that energy can neither be created or destroyed, only changed from one state into another. In this way, matter and energy can exchange forms with the form depending upon its vibrational frequency. Thus not only is the universe and all that is in it, including ourselves, based upon vibration, but our human thoughts, words, and emotions are also vibrational frequencies that vitally affect the quality of our lives.

Several colloquial phrases in the English language express the effects we feel of our vibrational frequency levels. For example, you say you're feeling "low" or "down in the dumps," or you're "on a high"—not the drug-related kind, of course.

Here's something to try: Think back to a time or event in which you were unhappy or fearful. As you do so, notice how you feel and how your body reacts. Now recall a wonderfully, happy time or event that made you feel elated. Again, notice the effects.

The kind of thoughts you had immediately affected how you felt and the wellbeing of your body, causing either a downward energy spiral or an uplifting, ascending frequency. No prize for guessing which one we all prefer! The point to remember is that persistent, low, vibrational frequencies lead to poor quality of life and ill health.

Laws of Vibration

To help you understand the underlying mechanism at work, here are the first three laws of vibrational science:

1. Lower vibrations can be reversed and raised if higher ones are applied. Higher frequencies rule.
2. But—and here's the challenge—once established, lower energy patterns will stay in place until they're acted upon for a long enough time by a higher frequency.
3. Lower vibrational frequencies persist longer and more easily than higher ones. This creates the tendency for recently raised vibrations to drop back to their longer-established levels. Unless the second law is applied continuously for a long enough period to make a permanent change, any benefit will only be temporary.

What does this tell you? Old habitual ways of thinking and living in a limited, lower third dimensional mindset lower your vibrations dramatically. The low frequency persists unless you determinedly and consistently apply a higher frequency perspective. The highest perspective you can apply is the certain knowing that your I AM HS is who you truly are and then choose to put it in charge of your life. You can maintain this high vibrational frequency by implementing the knowledge, understandings, and techniques in this book.

The mind cannot serve two masters. When you forget the true one, you falsely bow before the other. Mentally identifying with the physical or bodily realm lowers your vibrations so you see only a limited way of living, such as scarcity, ill health, and death. But when you mentally identify with your HS, you see only endless love, unlimited possibilities, and an abundance of every uplifting higher frequency manifestation and outcome, including miracles, exemplifying the highest vibrations that can occur in this material realm. The Law of Attraction—*like attracts like*—then ensures this becomes your ongoing reality for as long as you choose.

A Heaven on Earth life is achievable with the tools you're learning now. Simply pick yourself up when you fall back into old habits and replace them with the God-Effect.

Consider this sage advice: *Your day goes in the same direction as the corners of your mouth!*

Little Love Tip

Here's a quick pick-me-up tip to use when you notice your vibrational frequency is on a downward spiral:

The most potent vibration that quickly shifts a lower vibration upwards is when you're in a state of love. You can use any of love's many forms—compassion, joy, service, gratitude, blessing—to immediately raise your vibrational frequency.

And there's a wonderful health bonus too from maintaining states of love. Recent research shows that these states switch on more of our DNA-RNA codons which greatly increase health and immunity.

Your Three Minds

It may seem odd to say we have three minds, but it's not such an unfamiliar concept. You already subscribe, albeit unconsciously, to the fact that you have more than one mind when you say you are "of two minds" about something. But you actually have three minds, referred to as the *conscious*, *subconscious*, and *superconscious*, the last one referring to the Higher Mind of your I AM HS. The superconscious mind is an emanation of the Infinite Consciousness or Intelligence of the Divine Mind. All three are equally important, but so often the third one is overlooked. As you have just read, aligning and bringing your Higher Mind into play in your life is the difference between mediocrity and brilliance in the way you experience your life.

Your mind is your greatest tool and asset. Both ancient wisdom teachings and neuroscience agree that the mind operates through thoughts, understanding, reasoning and reflection or self-awareness. As your divinely-connected designing gift, your mind gives you the ability to dream up and clothe in form whatever thoughts you choose. Every focused thought carries within it the seed of creation or manifestation, and thoughts sent out into the physical realm can return like boomerangs as real things.

The Laws of Mind

Each thought can be likened to a river of a million sparking synapses, like a golden loom perpetually weaving and reweaving its way to a conclusion, is how eminent neuroscientist Sir John Eccles describes the power of our thoughts.

The Laws of Mind are partner to the Laws of Vibration because they profoundly affect everything you do every moment of every day and have the greatest influence on human life. When you consider how many thoughts the average person has each day, knowing how those thoughts operate and how to control them becomes essential if you want to consciously create a happier, healthier experience of life.

These laws are not new. In the scriptures it is written that "as a man thinketh, so is he." Buddha put it this way: "What we are today comes from our thoughts of yesterday, and our present thoughts build our life of tomorrow. Our life is the creation of our mind." Well worth thinking about!

If you'd like a more in-depth understanding of the Laws of Mind, I've explained how the nine main ones work in the Appendix. In the remainder of this chapter, I'll touch upon some of them to give you a sample of their significance.

Everything you do begins with a thought, whether in the form of an idea, a belief, or an inspiration. Then the decision follows whether to focus on that thought, take action and bring it into some kind of form or manifestation, or to attract the desired result to you. Success is won or lost in the mind. Negative thinking begets negative results, while positive thinking results in positive outcomes. Focusing on your limitations or excuses wastes valuable mental energy and power, while unknowingly creating more of the same. There's a saying which reminds us of this: *Argue for your limitations and they're yours.* You cannot think negative and positive thoughts at the same time, so it's a matter of *change the thought, change the outcome.*

Learning to control your mindset is paramount. Napoleon Hill, the American author and leader of the "New Thought" movement, explained this by saying that our thought impulses immediately begin to translate themselves into a physical equivalent, whether thoughts are voluntary—meaning conscious—or involuntary.

Hill realized that mind control is absolutely necessary. He explained that either you control your mind and thoughts, or they control you. There is no halfway compromise. But this requires the habit of mindfulness or awareness through constant evaluation and self-discipline.

Constantly ask yourself: *Are my current and consistent thoughts serving me? Or are they perpetuating my current situation? Are they giving me a good return on my time investment?* The secret habit of success is to keep your mind busy and occupied with definite purposes and goals, backed by definite plans. Without such control, success is not possible—nor are miracles.

Looking beyond current limited appearances into the realm of your divine potential frees you from the shackles that otherwise keep you bound to mediocrity and victimhood. Whatever you choose to accept as your reality and focus on becomes your reality. Are you dooming yourself to live with perceived external limitations by keeping your mind closed to the realm of unlimited possibilities? Like an umbrella, your mind only functions when it's open.

Your Next Step ...

Understanding your subconscious mind is a vital component of knowing who you are. But its influence goes beyond self-knowledge, because it has make-it or break-it power over how successful you are in manifesting the life you desire. Understanding your subconscious mind and its power is one of the important subjects of Step Two.

STEP II:

Breakthrough Keys on Your Path To Success

CHAPTER 5

KEY #1: Live the Life-Governing Universal Laws

How do we inadvertently turn off the miracle-working power of our HS? The analogy of an on/off power switch can help you to understand what is governing your outcomes. Think of plugging into a power source: if the switch is off, then nothing happens.

In this Step II, I present the five often unconscious causes that turn off the switch to your power source and block your manifestation mastery, with keys to turn that switch back on again. When you are in alignment with these keys, success of all kinds is possible. When you work against them, sadly failure will follow. Every power-blocker that stays active severely limits your Higher Self connection and short-circuits your chances for a successful outcome in what you wish to manifest.

Your supreme, unfailing I AM Higher Source can only bring or attract perfect outcomes into this dimension through you, if your power switches stay on. The good news is that no-one or nothing can turn them off—except you, yourself! You have absolute control, but only if you know how this works.

This first Key concerns the all-important Universal Laws of Life. You must understand exactly what these laws are and why they are so influential in human life.

Why Universal Laws Are Paramount

The Universal Laws of Life govern the spiritual and psychological life of every person on the planet. Being unaware they exist or not knowing how they apply to human existence dooms you to a less than satisfying life—permanently.

Regardless of whether you know about them or not, Universal Laws are immutable and remain in operation at all times similar to physical laws, such as gravity and aerodynamics, for example. You could say you don't believe in gravity, but if you jump off a high building, you'd certainly experience its effects directly.

Physical Universal laws govern all life in our known universe. They not only explain the way the universe and our third dimensional earth operate but also how all life is impacted by them.

Clearly, there could be no order in the universe without physical laws. It is similar with those laws that apply to human living. It's vitally important to knowingly align with and practise these laws, for life without law and order is a life of chaos and trouble, trial and error, hit and miss. These Universal Laws are also known as the Laws of Life or Natural Laws because they govern every person's life. But nothing can be really known by you unless you prove it. Merely to read or know the Universal Laws is not enough. You must use them to prove them. When you live and work aligned with these Laws, you know the outcome of every venture because their operation cannot fail.

Something important to remember yet often overlooked is that no one law can work in isolation. Just as you cannot bake a cake using only one ingredient, neither can you achieve success of any kind using only one law. When you choose to work with them together in perfect harmonious synergy, the results manifest in your life as your highest, natural, divine tendencies of love, peace, fulfilment, wellbeing, wisdom, contentment, power, truth, joy, perfection, harmony, strength, health, and abundance.

The word *law* derives from an Old Norse word meaning "something laid down or fixed," and the dictionary meanings include "a system of rules of action established by authority that regulate actions and have binding force or effect." Being of divine origin, the Universal Laws of Life or Light only express facts or truths—not beliefs, not someone's interpretation or opinion, but that which is factual truth. So many things that we loosely refer to as facts are instead our own or other people's interpretations, beliefs or opinions.

As you can see, the word itself indicates a law's unchanging quality. All laws are quite impartial and continue working at all times; being oblivious to them does not affect or diminish their action in any way. No-one can avoid or escape them. These unalterable laws are forever in action in your life and affairs in every single moment, governing and directing your consciously or unconsciously generated creations. Their consequences are evident in the quality of each person's daily life.

Neither you nor anyone else can consciously and rapidly evolve without knowledge and application of these laws. Only by understanding and then applying them to all the little things of your daily life can you learn to control then master your mental, emotional and physical bodies.

Life Mastery and Self-mastery begins with you consciously deciding to work in harmony with Universal Laws. Positive and pleasant events and results always occur as a result of living in alignment with them. Living in opposition to the laws, even inadvertently, results in less than enjoyable outcomes. Buddha taught that the cause of much of our pain and suffering is the violation of these universal laws.

Universal Laws provide the foundation for you to successfully tap into your latent power and potential. They are the difference between real success and freedom, or staying bound through ignorance to automatic responses or manipulation arising from the less evolved mass mind and belief systems.

The only way you can ever be absolutely certain of the Universal Laws far reaching effects is to integrate them into your life and see the difference they make. No-one can prove anything for you. No matter how many examples I or anyone else can give you to prove they work, it's still only hearsay to you, the reader.

Like wisdom, proof can't be taught, only experienced. Knowledge has to come first, followed by application. Then as you experience positive results you come to *know* rather than just believe the power of these guiding laws that empower you to live life outside and above the effects of the seductive mass consciousness. You're able to start living masterfully while still in human embodiment.

These simple yet profound laws act like brilliant lights shining away the darkness and no-sense of this "game of life" we play out on earth. As in any game, unless you know the rules of how to play, you can't ever hope to win or succeed, let alone enjoy the experience. Once you know the laws underpinning everything you think, feel and do, you are able to make certain and rapid progress—and have some fun at the same time.

Know your ABC's

What fundamental laws determine whether you become a manifestation master or not? Learning the ABC's, or first principles, of any subject is the necessary starting point. The following Universal Laws are the foundation of all success, so start by going through each one without judgment and recognize those that are personally relevant to you. As you integrate your understanding and correct any faulty mindset, you achieve another major breakthrough on your way to living the Miracle Effect.

As you read each of the ABC's, check to see whether it is your truth. If not, make it your own by stating in your own words a decree that incorporates each of your desired outcomes, as in the first example. Regularly repeating decrees as fact reprograms your subconscious mind, so it will support the success of all your desired outcomes.

- **A – Accept**. Can you honestly say: *I AM accepting that this outcome of _____ (what you desire to manifest) is possible, and I deserve it!*

  Make certain that you also accept without hesitation that miracles are possible too.

  I love how the Holy Spirit stated the *Law of Acceptance* some years ago as: "If you accept this, it's yours!" Great news in its positive interpretation, but conversely, if you can't fully accept that your perfect outcome is really possible, or if you hold even a smidgen of doubt, you activate the off switch instead of the on one. Similarly, if you accept someone else's negative belief, that, too, short-circuits your success. An example of this failure is when a doctor gives a patient a negative medical prognosis that can act as a death sentence, because in the doctor's understanding certain conditions are beyond hope.

Accepting the two principles of *possibility* and *being deserving* is the absolute fundamental first step, and leads to allowing yourself to receive perfect outcomes and miracles. Check both of these carefully within yourself and, if necessary, make the firm decision to replace all doubt with the fact that as a Divine Being anything is possible, and you are therefore worthy and deserving of having whatever you choose. Holding that thought, repeat the decree above with conviction until it's your truth.

- **B – Believe**. Can you truly say you believe that your perfect outcomes can and will manifest? Can you believe that you can achieve your goals—and miracles? As Henry Ford famously said, "Whether you think you can or think you can't, either way you're right." The *Law of Belief* states that whatever you believe is true—for you. You will make it so because your attitude drives your success, whether positive or negative. Believing equates with having faith, until you are able to upgrade *belief* to *knowing* through testing and proving it for yourself.

  This is one of the fundamental reasons for this book—to give you tools and understandings so you really can *know* rather than just hope or believe, that your life can be Heaven on Earth. I'm living proof of this. But I can't prove it for you. Only when you've done your own verifying, will you really know at a deep level. That's why I tell my students to be like spiritual scientists and follow scientific methodology: take what I've said as a premise, use and test it, then from the results that must be repeatable, you'll know whether it's valid or not.

- **C – Conceptualize** with **Certainty**. Napoleon Hill gave a famous formula: C + B = A, meaning whatever you can Conceive (or Conceptualize) and Believe, you can Achieve. This is another way of expressing the *Law of Certainty*. Once you're congruent with the limitless Power Source principle of your Higher Self, then the certainty of achieving your heart's desires is a given because it supersedes all other purely physical powers.

  The *Law of Certainty* goes hand in hand with the *Law of Cause and Effect*. You can be certain that the result you're aiming for will inevitably follow when you correctly put the relevant cause of that result into action. You are the cause of everything that happens in your life; your body and experiences are the effect. It's easier to blame people or things outside of yourself rather than take self-responsibility, but acknowledging yourself as the cause is part of the self-mastery journey.

- **C – Commitment**, meaning you'll follow through strongly and passionately. I'm paraphrasing part of Goethe's delightfully poetic way of stating this law:

  ... The moment you definitely commit yourself to your outcome, then Providence moves, too. All sorts of unexpected things happen to help you that would otherwise never have occurred. A whole cascade of events flows from the decision raising in your favor all manner of unforeseen incidents and

meetings, support and material assistance, which no-one could have imagined would, or even could, come your way.

I've proven this happens in so many diverse situations. One example is substantial financial donations given to me from time to time seemingly from "out of the blue" (or more correctly, "heaven sent"), supporting aspects of my Soul Service work to which I am totally committed. And they always come unsolicited at crucial times in particular projects, often at the last minute. Last year for example, I was organizing a conference to bring famous international teachers and authors from America to the New Zealand public. A few weeks out, however, much lower than expected registrations were making the conference's future look uncertain. I handed over the decision whether to continue or cancel the event to my Higher Self, letting go of all attachment as to which action to take.

Asking for others to give me help had not occurred to me, nor was it necessary. I simply placed the "order" for the perfect outcome to occur. HS took perfect care of the details. An unexpected, eleventh-hour major donation coming from "out of the blue" meant the event could go on. The human part of me is still stunned at the magnificence of working this way. You might be, too, once you experience it for yourself.

CHAPTER 6

KEY #2: Align with the Laws of Manifestation Mastery

Here's the next recipe of essential Universal Laws that through your everyday thoughts, words and actions must become automatic if you wish to keep your "on" power switch activated. In fact, the following four laws form a major part of the necessary foundation upon which to build your "diamond standard" extraordinary life. Living out of alignment with these laws will definitely flick your internal "off" switch and keep it off, making failure the outcome of your goals instead of success.

I suggest you take time to think about each law, first checking to ensure that you've accepted it as part of your basic mind-set. Then contemplate how you can weave each one's subtle power into your daily words and activities.

The Four Laws of Manifestation Mastery

1) *Law of Self Love.* This is not the ego-based kind of love but that which comes from knowing who you really are, a human of divine origin and connection. Self-love translates as self-worth and valuing yourself enough to know you deserve the best that life has to offer. (If self-love is a hard concept to accept straight away, I suggest you re-read Chapter 1 to fully integrate the magnificence of your real Self.)

Don't forget this law's partner, the *Law of Forgiveness.* Forgiveness is the flip side of love. You can't be in a state of love, the highest vibration known to humanity, without having forgiveness of others and yourself. Forgiveness has a dissolving power over the emotional effects of mistakes you or someone else has made, so those effects don't continue. Forgiveness doesn't mean you condone another's action or your own. It means that you let the actions and emotions go, so they stay in the past where they belong. Otherwise, they will continue their original effect, and taint the present and future. You know that you have truly forgiven when you can bless the other person by remembering their Divine Self rather than their lower-self action. As the Dalai Lama so beautifully puts it: "Separate the action from the person." In relation to yourself, forgive yourself if you've ever acted in an unloving or selfish way, or when you've ever thought of yourself as anything but divine.

2) *Law of Appreciation and Gratitude.* This is a law of increase fundamental on so many levels. Daily giving thanks for all the good and wonderful things in your life past, present and future, keeps your vibrational frequencies high by holding your focus only on the positive. It also sends a powerful psychological signal to your subconscious mind. Focusing on what you do enjoy and already have in your life, turbo-charges your creative power. By giving it energy to keep it alive and active, you keep the energies flowing to expand, increase, and maintain everything you're enjoying. I'm sure you've heard the truism: *Where your focus goes, the energy flows.*

Appreciation and holding a grateful attitude actually does a lot of other important things as well. It doesn't matter who or what you choose to appreciate, the effect is the same. You can feel appreciation for your loved ones, for loyal and supportive friends and their acts of kindness (don't forget those who have passed on), your animals, your body, nature or even such things as your computer—anything that helps to make your life so blessed. The main thing to remember is to give thanks often throughout each day. Especially appreciate your I AM Higher Self and be grateful for your life experience.

Going from the sublime to the basic, I was most amused to hear the late Dr. Wayne Dyer admit to doing the same thing I've been doing for years—giving thanks for my body's essential functioning every time I go to the bathroom!

German mystic philosopher Meister Eckhart said if the only prayer you ever pray is *thank you,* that would be enough. When you say *Amen,* you're saying thank you. Saying grace at a meal is giving thanks for the food. Physiologically, because your vibrational rate goes up whenever you're in a state of appreciation, it helps to keep your body healthy as well as reducing stress. You'll feel better because it signals your brain to release "feel-good" endorphins.

Modern research is showing that people who are generally more appreciative live longer. They actually get sick less often, and if they do, they heal faster. On top of this, their relationships are better and last longer. That's just some of the internal stuff that's good for you. Externally, when you appreciate somebody else, it creates a vibrational shift in them as well. Just say to anyone, *I really love you* or *I appreciate what you did*, and watch the person's face light up.

3) Law of Oneness or Unity Consciousness states that if you truly understand your connectedness as being a member of one human family, whatever you desire for yourself you will automatically desire for everyone else. This is selflessness in action, which is also a blessing to all humanity. Remembering this law leads to the realization that whatever you do has a flow-on effect to the whole body of humanity, all life-forms—and the environment.

4) Law of Enthusiasm or Excitement adds the heat to cook the recipes for success. How confirming to find the word *enthusiasm* comes from the Greek word for "God within." Because of its high vibrational frequencies, this law together with joy or joyful anticipation provides the *oomph* that accelerates all your outcomes. Their action is rather like the leavening agent in bread, or like putting more logs on the fire to increase the heat. So unless you want your manifestation results to be half-baked, remember to imagine what it will feel like when you are enjoying your successful outcome. Get enthused with anticipation right from the moment you set your goal.

Think back to a time when you were excited, even passionate about something. Not only did you feel more vibrantly alive, but your whole enjoyment of life went to another level. Such a positive state of mind made sure you kept your focus, thus energizing the outcome you desired.

CHAPTER 7

KEY #3: Change Unwanted Subconscious Mental Programs

The first major self-sabotaging cause that prevents your success in manifesting what you would like comes from negative mind programs installed in your subconscious from birth. Some mind programs are taken on board from people you accept as being more knowledgeable than you or an authority in some area or role. But the majority are the result of circumstances and conditionings in your early childhood that reflect the experiences, limited thinking, emotions and beliefs of others.

Such mind programs come from people who surrounded you in your formative years, be they parents, caregivers, representatives of the culture, religion, education or political system you were born into. Therefore they are other people's belief patterns, whether positive or negative, that you have unknowingly accepted as true. They become your beliefs and remain in operation until you look at them and decide whether or not they are true for you now, and whether you wish to hold on to them.

For example, think of the expressions that tend to pepper your conversations without you thinking about what you are saying. For example, do you say things like, *Oh that's so expensive, I can't afford that,* resulting in your shopping being automatically ruled by price above all else? I'm not suggesting that bargains aren't good, but such words and actions reflect underlying beliefs that you learned from others and may not be true for you now.

I remember hearing these expressions myself throughout most of my life, along with phrases like having to "scrimp and scrape" to make ends meet. Even when financial circumstances eventually eased for my parents and their friends, the beliefs remained, so they continued to limit themselves. It's surprising how many disempowering beliefs we hold at the subconscious level.

It wasn't until I understood the power beliefs have over the quality of a person's life that I decided to question my own, one by one, and see which were true for the way I was now choosing to view my life. Only then was I in the position of being able to delete them and replace them with what was my informed reality—in other words, to take my personal power back. Returning to the earlier example, the only remnant of that shopping consciousness I'm deliberately choosing to hold on to is buying specials on basic items I always have in my pantry—but the difference is that I do it *consciously.*

Another example is a dear friend repeatedly expressing her fear that she won't have enough money to "put food on the table" for herself and three adult children. Such belief patterns are the foundation of notions such as *Life is a struggle, There's not enough to go round,* or *Bottom line, it's all up to poor, little me.* It takes a completely different understanding to change limiting mindsets and hence your life.

Your subconscious mind also works as a personal life experience recording and playback system. It is faithfully recording every single thing you think, believe, feel and do, something it has been doing since birth. Since it cannot reason or discern what is good or bad for you, it simply records everything as belief patterns. No matter what you as an adult set out to create, your subconscious programs control the end result being successful or not. This is because its only power is of deduction, so it obeys without question all that has been recorded and installed. It sets about creating real-life scenarios and experiences deduced from your input, whether conscious or unconscious in origin, that confirm your beliefs. In other words, it ensures your end result matches your belief programs. This is where the problem lies, and it explains why at times no matter how hard you try, you just can't seem to manifest what you consciously want in spite of applying all the means and tools you know.

Compounding this is the fact that the subconscious mind's play-back function also acts rather like a non-stop personal search engine. Moment by moment, your mind is searching and then identifying everything recorded within its vast memory storage system that corresponds to whatever thought, feeling or motivation you're focusing on in any given moment. Whatever else matches is then brought to the surface, as it were. Seamlessly, your subconscious mind immediately activates these installed memory patterns and beliefs, so their added energies also influence the final result of your conscious focus. Little wonder then that so many plans fail, and goals aren't achieved.

Perhaps you can see how this has affected your own hoped-for results in the past. I like to think of it as pressing the bold key when writing on my computer: whatever I type is highlighted. That is, until I turn it off. Similarly, knowing what's going on below the conscious level puts you into a position of being able to de-activate what would otherwise be 'highlighted,' and so change your success rate for the better. The good news is that this process works the same if a program is based upon a previous positive experience or belief, because it then supports you in achieving a successful and positive outcome.

Neuroscience tells us that the subconscious mind is running by default 95 percent of the time. That's because the only time you are in complete control is the 5 percent when you're consciously focused on something specific. As soon as you switch to everyday thoughts and distractions, the subconscious patterns kick in and take over. If they're not supportive ones, they effectively sabotage all your efforts. This fact alone highlights how imperative it is that you recognize and change or delete unwanted subconscious mental programs, something I'll be addressing later in this chapter and in Step IV.

Victim or Victor

Another insidious emotional culprit that's very prevalent today is victim-consciousness. If seeded into a person's subconscious mind by the beliefs of those they grew up with, victim consciousness becomes a bad habit. You can hear it in the many commonly used expressions, even some you may hear yourself saying, like: *I'm always so unlucky. If anything bad is going to happen, it will happen to me. Whatever can go wrong will go wrong. Just my luck! Why me?* and so on.

With this kind of programming, you live in a constant level of fear-based stress, wondering what's just around the corner waiting to happen to you. *Will I have good luck or bad luck?* is the question never far out of your mind, but fearing the worst. Obviously any version of this belief system keeps power switches in the off position. And as already explained, the ego will obediently play out situations again and again that confirm such beliefs.

Some years ago when I was facilitating a spiritual discussion group, I witnessed the effects of victim-consciousness play out dramatically. We had been talking about how we create our reality, and over a cup of tea I happened to say in passing that unless of karmic origin, most of the usual negative life situations don't have to be experienced. One of the ladies put down her cup and looked at me with obvious disbelief.

"That's impossible," she vehemently retorted, stifling a derisive snort as she turned away. "You can't avoid bad things happening."

We weren't too surprised by her response, as this person often talked about how down on her luck she was and how life was so unfair. Sadly, within the following few months a series of negative events confirmed her negative beliefs: her husband of over 20 years announced one Sunday without any warning that the marriage was over and left on the Tuesday; her car was stolen for a second time; she unsurprisingly had a bout of illness; and then she had a house fire that destroyed the whole top floor of her home. We all rallied round to help and support her, but after she moved away from the area, I wondered whether she was able to change her thought patterns and negative beliefs so such distressing events didn't recur. I do hope so.

Recognize Your Unwanted Subconscious Beliefs

Are you doomed to remain a victim of negative thoughts and belief programs lurking below the surface of your mind, unrecognized yet subtly controlling the outcomes of your life? Absolutely not. The little quiz below on core beliefs that have far-reaching effects, will help you recognize if some fundamental changes are necessary to delete self-sabotaging programs. Up ahead, Step IV gives you precise ways to identify even more negative mindsets that aren't serving you, and working with the empowering information and techniques in this book will, without doubt, clear many more.

As a starting point to help you recognize a few all-pervasive, limiting subconscious beliefs you may also unknowingly be holding that are common to many people, see what your reactions are to the following statements. I suggest you read each one out loud and then allow your intuitive answer to pop into your mind.

To help you get maximum benefit from this exercise, you can rate your answers from 0 to 5, with 0 representing "never" and 5 representing the absolute truth for you.

What is your immediate reaction to:

1. I AM lovable and much loved. _____
2. I AM worthy and deserve boundless love and loving relationships. _____
3. I AM fulfilled and content. _____
4. I AM successful. _____
5. I AM glowing with vitality and enthusiasm. _____
6. I AM radiating wellbeing. _____
7. I AM rejuvenating and forever young. _____
8. I AM effortlessly manifesting great abundance, including money. _____
9. I AM incredibly wealthy. _____
10. I AM all I can be, a perfect expression of my Divinity. _____

Did these statements resonate as true for you? Or did some make you feel uncomfortable? If so, these are valuable clues to what is running in your subconscious.

Those you rated 4 or 5 mean you have mostly positive and empowering subconscious belief programs about yourself, and so you're able to or are already manifesting these truisms. Well done! You have been fortunate enough to be exposed to these highly empowering truths probably from a young age, so give thanks to those who gave them to you.

A rating of 2 or 3 suggests you have mixed beliefs and conditioning about your potential, resulting in mixed success and outcomes around these aspects. As we go on, you'll gain understandings for how to improve your ratings.

Flag those you rated 1 or 0. These indicate that up until now you've been sadly limited by belief in that statement's complete opposites. They indicate the underlying causes of those areas of your life that you're no doubt ready to change for the better.

The ultimate goal is to be able to state each one as your truth, with conviction and without a shred of doubt. Replacing them with certainty of your true Self and implementing the essential Laws of the Universe will effectively do just that.

When I recognize a belief I'm running, my criteria is to ask myself: Is it serving me? Does it enhance my life or make me feel happier, more peaceful, confident and lighter? Or does it cause me to feel lacking, not good or worthy enough, worried, fearful, concerned about people, situations arising, the future—in other words, a victim? This immediately provides the motivation to do something about it and so change my reality.

CHAPTER 8

KEY #4: Examine Fear, Stress, Worry, and Anxiety

Now let's look at major "off" switches of the emotional kind. As you'll have seen from the quiz you took in Chapter 7, feelings are based upon beliefs recorded in your subconscious mind. Negative feelings arise from the mistaken beliefs that are lurking there unnoticed.

Emotions and beliefs arise from thoughts—thinking makes them so. Although you may not be aware of the original thoughts that produced the negative sabotaging beliefs, they have a common denominator: *fear*. Fear arises from an absence of trust in your Higher Power, usually through ignorance of the truth that because of your divine origin you must have unlimited potential to express all possible divine attributes freely and with ease. Trust is a natural result of living in a state of spiritual Love, and according to *A Course in Miracles*, love's opposite is not hate but fear.

Fear: The Opposite of Love

Fear is the absence of love, just as darkness is the absence of light. Spiritual Love creates trust, inner peace and fearlessness—and a life of freedom. What are we actually afraid of? For many people, fear stems from deep-seated, subconscious emotions, such as not feeling good enough or worthy, fear of failing or being judged, fear of being unlovable or unloved. Knowing and accepting your true Self is the antidote to all of them.

When you are afraid, all you are doing is covering your back. What happens physically is that fear centres energy in the *amygdala*, the area in the middle of your brain where fears can live and thrive, taking over and paralyzing your ability to think clearly. When you are relaxed however, the energy goes to the *prefrontal cortex* area of your brain where rational decision-making occurs. Only when you're not afraid can you look at a situation calmly and make a rational decision or choice—and receive higher guidance.

The prefrontal cortex is also the area in the brain where spiritual insights occur, which is why the third eye chakra is located there. When you meditate, you are using third eye power to focus your energy into that prefrontal cortex, which wakes up the enlightenment potential of your human self.

Repetitive thinking about fear in any form is unproductive and can actually attract what you are afraid of into your life because you're giving it life and energy. Or if you're fearful of something not happening, then you actually push it away rather than helping it to manifest.

Fear expresses as three of the most common and debilitating emotions—stress, worry and anxiety.

Stress: Identify the Fear

If you track the condition of being stressed, you end up with a cause for that stress that is an aspect of fear. This may be fear of lack, of being out of control, of not performing or living up to someone else's standards or expectations—or your own self-imposed ones. Another cause of stress is around time limitations, for example feeling there's not enough time for doing or achieving something. If you give any of these causes of your stress some quiet, calm thought, you'll no doubt realize that both self-imposed parameters and those from other people are completely arbitrary.

If you step back and choose not to be bound by such fears, does it really create a life-threatening situation or one without a solution? Very, very rarely. This realization helps you put your fear into perspective and move your energy back to your prefrontal cortex, so you can assess the circumstance from a rational viewpoint and come up with a solution. Most importantly, it enables you to consciously release the stress and tension that would otherwise take over and rule your life. And remember to breathe deeply while mentally handing over the cause of your stress to your Higher Self source of power. Meditation has now been proven beyond doubt to be one of the most powerful de-stressing solutions of all.

When you feel stressed how does your body react? You tense up often from head to toe. The eyes, jaw, teeth and scalp may tense, shutting off the free flow of health-giving energy, thus affecting your thinking and problem-solving. If prolonged, this often results in headaches or migraines. Neck tension and hunched shoulders are common symptoms, too, which inhibit the vital cranial-sacral flow necessary for good health of mind and body. Other reactions are when you feel uptight or your stomach feels knotted—you know the expression, *feeling sick in the stomach*. It's well researched how the brain under prolonged stress overproduces an inflammatory hormone, *cortisol*, that is the cause of a number of physical ailments.

Not so well known is that a form of acid is also produced under stress that floods the body, creating an acidic environment. Acid thoughts equal an acidic body, and create the environment that arthritis and cancer need to thrive. Guilt is another great stressor that causes anxiety with similar effects. The remedy that neutralizes this is forgiveness which I discussed in Key #3 in Chapter 7.

To sum up, to release or at least lower your stress levels, aim to identify the underlying fear cause, so you are then in a position to re-program your thinking and change the way you view the situation. As an example, a few years ago a friend and graduate student of mine was unexpectedly made redundant at her workplace along with a number of her colleagues. They took it very hard, so much so, many needed counseling—all except my friend who took in cakes for morning tea the following day to celebrate. She looked upon the change as an exciting opportunity to go in a different direction. No prize for guessing who quickly found the next most perfect career move!

Remember, emotions are under the control of your mind, so using your mind is the primary means of resolving any emotional problem. The other important point to remember is that what you focus on is more likely to become reality because of the truth that where your attention goes, the energy flows.

Why Worry?

More often than not, stress builds up from prolonged worry or anxiety. Worry is wasted emotion, and yet how many people stop and ask themselves if worrying about someone or something is actually helping the situation? The fact is that worrying doesn't help in any way whatsoever. It clouds the mind and adversely affects the health and wellbeing of the worrier, while making him or her less capable of helping another person or themselves, or being able to assist in resolving or defusing a situation. Worrying is like sitting in a rocking chair; it keeps you very busy but goes nowhere.

Most worrying is based upon fear of the future, known as *what-ifs*. Yet if you look back at what you were worrying about last month, last year—how many what-if scenarios actually happened? Often the causes of this kind of worry are to do with thinking, *What if I let someone—or myself— down? What if I do or can't do this or that? What will people think of me if I say or do this?* Remember the self-esteem basis of fear?

At work, the what-if may be time-based—*What if I don't meet a certain deadline, complete what's expected of me?* The irony is that worrying about such things actually slows you down and makes you less productive. Far better to remember that your boss is a human being too, whom, if you talk to about your concern will most likely understand and help you out. If not, perhaps it's a good time to ask yourself why you're still in that job.

The other big thing that causes so many people to worry is money, or more precisely the fear of not having enough for their needs. I discuss this at length in Chapter 17 and include ways I have proven to help you become a "money magnet." Real freedom comes from looking squarely at the things that bother you and delving into their real causes rather than their surface appearances. Then, instead of allowing them to dominate your thoughts and life, spend your time working on ways that enable you to transcend them and their effects. The good news is that by reading this book, you're already well on the way to doing this.

The Dalai Lama, a wonderful living example of an enlightened human, sums up the solution to eradicating worry beautifully and succinctly this way: *If you're worrying about something that can be fixed, why worry? If you're worrying about something that cannot be fixed, why worry?*

Eastern sages have long known the effects of stress, worry and anxiety. Wisely they observed that prolonged stress and its partner worry are the reasons many people die at a relatively young age: they use up the second half of their life in the first. A sobering thought.

Be Aware of Your Negative Emotions

You'll find many stress-busting tools and techniques throughout this guidebook, but the trick lies in making time to slot some of these practical antidotes into your everyday life. By keeping calm, you can learn to be pro-active rather than reactive, and be on the alert to noticing any change in your stress levels. If they start rising, immediately do something to defuse them rather than succumb to a reactive response. This way you learn to live consciously above the stress-worry belt and stay in the driver's seat.

Leonardo da Vinci once observed that people of accomplishment rarely sat back and let things happen to them. They went out and happened to things. And Joseph Campbell observed that opportunities to find deeper powers within ourselves come when life seems most challenging. A little jingle that helps me remember the truth about stress and its effects is this: *In a relaxed happy state, I can create. When under stress, I have much less.*

Check to see if stress, worry, or anxiety, tend to be part of your life on a regular basis. Once you are aware of them, you can then de-activate them as they arise and before their unwelcome effects take over. Not only do negative emotions (no matter how fleeting) stop progress dead in its tracks, but they also impact how you view and experience life. And they neurologically impede your capacity to realize your full God-given potential.

If you find yourself getting caught up in any of these negative thoughts or emotions, remember the quickest antidote to reversing any downward spiraling vibrational frequency is to smile. Or better still, find something to laugh at. I always have a book of jokes handy that, even if I don't actually need for a quick fix, I enjoy re-reading anyway. There's also a wonderful saying that helps others as well as yourself: *If you see someone without a smile, give them one of yours.*

CHAPTER 9

KEY #5: De-activate Seed Causes and Clear Karmic Debt

Have you ever worked on creating or attracting something into your life and no matter what positive techniques you used, it still never eventuated?

In this chapter, we explore two more possible deep-seated reasons for such failure: *past life seed causes* and *past life karma*. These causes are based upon the concept of reincarnation meaning your current life is but the latest in a long, ongoing line of returning in different physical embodiments to experience different life circumstances and possibilities. Each lifetime gives you the opportunity to right any wrongs you may have previously committed and learn from them. This is known as karma, the personal cause and effect scenarios you created.

Deeply-hidden seed causes arise from imperfect thinking, beliefs or conclusions drawn from negative incidents that you experienced or created in your past lives. All were recorded in your soul and are known as your Akashic records. In future incarnations, these usually create sabotaging programs that often mystify until put into this context. The underlying energy of these patterns is carried forward into the subconscious mind each life-time, there to await recognition and clearing.

These seed causes act like the software of your subconscious bio-computer mind. No matter what you try and do, if it's not in agreement with your software program, then there is no way you will get the results you want. You have to change or delete the causes at the source because the ego very obligingly plays out subconscious patterns as mindsets and no amount of conscious work can over-ride them. Sadly, until you become aware enough, such mindsets go unrecognized, except perhaps when you notice limiting or unpleasant situations that keep recurring.

Obstacles in life can be created by the ego as it obediently out-pictures past-life seed causes. If the obstacles impede your spiritual development, they may require your Higher Self's help to overcome. To make this point, I often ask my audience at the start of a major life-changing seminar or spiritual event how many people were faced with situations that challenged their determination to attend. You'd be amazed at how many hands go up. Fortunately, I've noticed that in most cases the Higher Self intervenes enough to get folks where they know, at their soul level, they're meant to be. But to get the full, ongoing benefit of any self-work, they still have to erase the seed causes to ensure they don't reappear at a later date.

Such seed causes are usually based upon soul memories of failure or religious indoctrination in previous lives that created feelings of not being capable, deserving or worthy enough for spiritual progress. Difficulties then present themselves in this life that confirm the mistaken beliefs. Seeing beyond the outer form rather than being influenced by apparent deterrents makes it possible to overcome such challenges.

Following is an HS-inspired technique to rid yourself of sabotaging seed causes once and for all:

De-activating and Replacing Seed Causes

1. **First you must de-activate the seed cause, and then any further effects by deleting any record of it continuing.** This is done by stating a firm decree. A decree is different than an affirmation because a decree leaves no room for doubt, whereas an affirmation or ordinary hopeful statement inherently contains an element of "maybe." A decree on the other hand, especially when you invoke your I AM HS, indicates you *know*, not just believe or hope, that it is already done because you are imprinting it on the Quantum Field as well as in your own consciousness. You can make up your own decrees, but here's a suggestion to get you started:

   With the Power of my I AM HS, I decree that the seed cause from this or any lifetime that has up until now prevented my desired outcome of _____ is now permanently de-activated. I AM pressing the delete button, and I AM permanently erasing its cause, record, memory and effects (including the normal prognosis or expected progression if it's to do with self-healing). It is already done.

2. **Replace the de-activated seed cause with a positive decree for your desired outcome.** For example:

   With the Power of my I AM HS, I decree that my perfect outcome of _____ is already accomplished in the Quantum Field, and I AM bringing it into physical manifestation now.

Always put the desired outcome in the past instead of in the future, so you can enjoy it now in the present. As the saying goes, *Tomorrow never comes*!

If your outcome is for health, rejuvenation, self-healing and/or wellbeing, add the intention that the original, perfect God-Code Blueprint in your DNA is activated. This worked for me when I included this decree in the self-healing of my two degenerative bone conditions. (To understand the DNA Divine Code concept better, see Appendix item *The God Code in Your DNA*. If you're interested in learning about this in greater detail, I highly recommend Gregg Braden's book *The God Code*.)

3. **In your mind, change** your thoughts about how your situation or condition was previously doomed to progress, into how your perfect outcome will now be manifesting the way you'd like it to be. Imagine yourself enjoying the result, feel how wonderful life is with the replacement in operation instead—and remember to give thanks to HS that *it is so.*

Past Life Karma

Although I've discussed the most obvious mindset and emotional blocks needing to be addressed, one other deeply-embedded possibility remains, which is *past life karma*.

On occasion, the outcome you desire is not in alignment with a karmic experience that you—your soul and Higher Self—have chosen to experience. In order to balance or clear something you did that caused suffering to another in a previous life, the inescapable but perfectly just Law of Karma ensures that you take appropriate action or experience something similar yourself. The analogy is that you have a debt that must be paid.

For example, let's suppose that prior to incarnating, you chose to clear a debt during this lifetime of deliberately causing another person to suffer through lack or deprivation. Perhaps the way you chose to clear this karma is to experience for yourself what that kind of suffering feels like, or how it limits your life. Therefore, in the context of wishing to manifest abundance, your pre-incarnation decision will prevent you from doing so, no matter how well you apply the tools. This is only a simple generalization to illustrate the principle because every karmic choice and incident is perfectly played out through situations created by your soul and Higher Self.

The good news is that when a karmic-based situation occurs, it doesn't have to be a permanent state. Once you recognize or accept that the experience may be karmic in origin, opportunities to create beneficial situations that help others and express its polar opposite arise. In addition, through applying the Law of Forgiveness to heal any suffering you caused—and to forgive yourself—you are able to clear many karmic debts. (I've included a powerful Forgiveness Decree that helps this process in the Appendix.)

The more you clear these discordant, lower frequency energies accumulated over countless lifetimes, the greater access you will have to your Higher Power which can then flow into your life in greater and greater intensity.

One more important point to note is that no one else can clear your karmic debts for you, seeing you were the one who created them. And it's a relief to know that you cannot take on anyone else's karmic responsibilities, either.

Your Next Step ....

Knowing these Keys to remove all obstacles in your path to mastery success is crucial for you to become a Miracle Me. Now you are ready to move forward and unlock the secrets to living Heaven on Earth with the Miracle Effect fully active in your every day life.

STEP III:

How To Unlock the Secrets of Your Success

CHAPTER 10

Master Secret #1: Restore Your Divine Power Technique

Are you ready to master the secrets for successfully living the Miracle Effect? For real and lasting success, you have to actually *use* the principles that govern miracle mastery, both *experimentally* and experientially.

There are many talking heads, speakers and sages who can give a lecture about their philosophy, and while interesting, talks rarely change lives on a permanent basis. This guidebook on the other hand, details clear, step-by-step processes and techniques developed and distilled from my past 40 years' research and practice in forms that easily imprint them into your memory and consciousness. Once embodied and applied rather than just intellectually understood, they guarantee your success.

As the first master secret for cultivating the Miracle Effect, the process I'm sharing is a powerful, inner activation technique that has an immediate, high-voltage result that is permanent. This unique process was given to me by my Higher Self as an effective way to dramatically increase vibrational frequency and power-up your inner Light quotient. Doing it regularly keeps your inner energy network permanently activated, so you can quickly reverse any drop in your vibration.

Axiatonal Lines Restoration

The term *axiatonal lines* was introduced by Dr. J J Hurtak in his mind-opening book, *The Book of Knowledge:*

The Keys of Enoch, in Key 317. Once restored and activated, axiatonal lines are energetic and vibratory lines that extend from your acupuncture meridians to connect directly with the primary Light blueprint of your I AM Overself. This means your whole being, right down to your DNA-RNA, can be vibrationally upgraded through the hugely increased Higher Source energy flow.

Axiatonal or Axial lines connecting with your Overself form a grid network within your body that's also aligned with the Light cable of your spinal column and its chakras. Today, most of humanity exists with only remnants of what these lines once were, providing a minimal trickle of life-energy.

For a visual, think of neon signs that are almost unseen until the power switch is flipped. Only when full power is restored do they light up. Imagine your axial lines as an unlit grid whose great power potential you can activate through the process I share with you below.

The results are observable in more than one way. Recently I met a very tuned-in lady who, although she didn't mention it at the time, made this observation in an email she sent me the following day: *You have an interesting structure in your body— a laser- gold light grid!*

The added beauty of this unique activation process is that it enables you to be re-programmed by your I AM Overself. Such powerful help greatly supports your ultimate goal of freedom from physical slavery to third-dimensional consciousness and all its limitations. Powerful stuff!

Sacred Geometry, Chakras, and Divine Names

Incorporated in the process for maximum effectiveness are universal symbols of sacred geometry, the chakra system, and physical actions necessary for mind-body integration.

All become unified and "powered up" by the use of divine names in the language of Light.

The sacred geometry symbols used are triangles and the diamond that is the inner core of the star tetrahedron.

Triangles and star tetrahedrons are part of our very make-up. Their pyramidal fields are found, for example, in blood crystals and hydrogen atoms, while the energy field of water is in the form of a star tetrahedron. Both the planet and our bodies are made up of around 70 per cent water, so this sacred geometry is energetically an intrinsic part of us.

Chakras are the seven energetic spinning vortices situated along your spinal cord. They are radiating and receiving energy centers that act as portals between spiritual, mental and biological networks of your physical body.

Chanting the supreme divine name of *Yod-Heh-Vod-Heh* written as YHWH (in ancient Hebrew our W is pronounced as a V), helps to imprint its incredibly powerful vibrational frequencies into your physical form. This occurs with continual, focused chanting and visualization by activating your dormant inner Light Body.

Tapping actions are used on several important acupuncture and intersecting axial points to activate physical and neurological integration. They are done three times in each place—think of a bedside touch-activated lamp that requires three taps to turn it on from low to full light power. Most of humanity is existing on the lowest level of energy flowing from their I AM Higher Selves, which is just enough to stay alive, so this process is like turning up the dimmer switch to full.

Process to Restore Your *Axiatonal Grid*

Here are directions to restore and activate your axiatonal grid within your physical body, and turn up the dimmer switch of your inner Light.

Begin by bringing your hands from above your head down towards the 7th Crown Chakra at the top of your head.

CHAKRA	*WORD*	*ACTION*	
7th Crown -	YOD ... Hands form diamond - (centre of Star Tetrahedron) at the chakra vortex		
	HEH ... Open hands to sides at eye level, creating an energy triangle		
6th 3rd Eye -	VOD/VAV ... Hands form an upward triangle at the chakra vortex		
	HEH ... Tap your temples 3 times to link right and left brain hemispheres and acupuncture intersections		
5th Throat -	YOD ... Hands form an upward triangle at the chakra vortex		
	HEH ... Tap shoulders to link with acupuncture intersections		
4th Heart -	VOD/VAV ... Hands form a diamond at the heart chakra		
	HEH ... Open arms to side at right angles which is the Sign of Transformation position: l_o_l		
3rd Solar Plexus -	YOD ... Hands form a downward triangle at chakra vortex		

HEH ... Extend triangle as you tap the top of your pelvis

2nd Sacral - VOD ... Hands form a downward triangle at chakra vortex

HEH ... Tap hip joints to link with acupuncture intersections

1st Base - YAH ... Hands form a diamond at root chakra, then extend hands and continue saying *YAH (the short version of YHWH)* as you visualize secondary knee chakras, then feet chakras, while directing the energy flow down to earth to ground yourself – as shown in the two arrows

Bring hands upwards, rotating in "As above, so below" positions (see diagram) to a repeated chant of *'Ehyeh Ain Soph Aur'* (pronounced: *'ay yea (rhyming with hay) ane (like rain) sof oor (like pure),*meaning 'I AM Limitless Light,'until you can extend arms upwards and outwards in a V, ready to repeat the whole process at least twice more.

To fully integrate and imprint this process into your consciousness and body, repeat all steps in detail for a minimum of 33 times over a period of time.

Once fully integrated, you can do this quick version to maintain your full axiatonal lines power flow:

Let your hands flow down your body in wave form, crossing at each chakra (as in diagram), visualizing each restoration point. Use the same chant of *YHWH* three times plus *YAH*. The goal is to be able to do this physically every day, or in your mind without using your hands.

Using the most powerful of divine names, *YHWH*, and the out breath of *YAH,* raises your vibrational frequency and super-charges activation of any process far beyond what any third-dimensional words could ever do. (*Note*: While you are learning the process, it may help if you remember that every *YOD* and *VOD/VAU* you chant occurs when your hands are at a chakra point on the body. On every *HEH* your hands are at a side position or off the body.)

I've found that ultimately what began as three vertical YHWHs merges into one blazing, symbolic Light Body form, overlaying and imprinting my whole physical being and consciousness. No wonder the tuned-in lady who sent me an email saw my body structure as *a laser-gold light grid.* Try restoring your own axiatonal lines with this process and experience for yourself how the powerful flow of energy lights *you* up!

CHAPTER 11

Master Secret #2: Maintain Your Full Power & Energy Flow

You have already gained power through understanding who you truly are, knowing how to remember your true nature, and having an activating process to restore your full flow of energy from your I AM Higher Overself. As you strengthen the God-Effect of daily remembering this knowledge, you may be sensing a subtle glow radiating from within, even greater than the feeling of wellbeing generates.

Now let's look at how you can maintain the high-powered energy of this Love Light-filled state every day. I find the following routine works most effectively for me, but you can create your own routine if you prefer. Choose the order of the following components that you feel are essential for optimum results for your way of life.

Making Each Day GREAT

Today even business success gurus are stressing how important it is to start each day in the best possible way. It's encouraging to see this concept becoming mainstream, and their suggestions, though from a secular viewpoint, are very close to my own. Here is my version that I use without fail to start each day in the most perfect way:

G – Gratitude. As soon as I wake up, I give thanks by saying something like, *I'm so happy and grateful for my night's sleep, my comfortable bed, for the gift of this new day with all its possibilities including miracles, for the Heaven on Earth life I enjoy.*

R – Reason. I bring to mind what I'm choosing to make my purpose or mission for this day, even if it's to take a day off and enjoy myself. My dear mother, who lived into her hundredth year, was a wonderful example of this. She remained active and useful almost to the end when her heart valve wore out, and when people asked her for her secret, the answer she gave was to have a purpose for waking up each day, something to look forward to.

E – Enthusiasm and Excitement. I am enthusiastic and excited for what the day may bring and for what I can accomplish and _e_njoy. This _e_nergizes me and reminds me to smile, rather like unwrapping a present.

A – Ask. I ask HS how best I may serve this day, as well as—*How can I be more loving and caring?* And most importantly, as the business gurus also stress, A is for avoiding opening emails until later in the day, unless your life or work depends upon timing. Otherwise, you allow others to take over your day. For me, I don't open my computer until after midday.

T – Time to Tune-Up. I take time for myself to set the tone of my day. If you have a very busy lifestyle, remember to prioritize your time so you can accomplish your projects without stress. I use the following two tune-up techniques followed by taking time for contemplation and meditation.

Tuning My Instrument

If you've ever heard a violin or piano played that hasn't been tuned, you'll appreciate my analogy of "tuning my instrument"—the *instrument* being my mind and body. We are constantly bombarded with the mass consciousness of humanity's thoughts and emotions, the media, and our own daily life interactions. This puts us "off key," so I like to start each day bringing myself back into alignment with my I AM HS. You'll be amazed at the difference it makes in how your days unfold when you use these techniques:

Divine Name Chanting. I tune my instrument by chanting the divine name of *Yod – Heh – Vod – Heh* 12 times. This is one of, if not *the* most powerful names of the Creator in the language of Light whose vibratory frequency surpasses all others. Remember, intention together with feeling and visualization of your desired result, are the necessary activation keys for any technique, especially when chanting. Here's how I do it:

- For the first six times I chant, I focus on the limitlessness Love-Light of Divine Creation of which my I AM Higher Self Light body is an expression. I bring to mind the enormity of this simple yet profound truth that reinforces my limitless, divine potential awareness at a deep level. Sometimes I add this to particular outcomes I may be focusing on, or simply to boost their Higher Power component.

  Reading the Divine Name   ה ו ה י

  Heh Vod Heh Yod

  as I chant it provides an optical mantra as an added bonus—Hebrew reads from right to left.

- For the second six times I chant this all-inclusive divine Name, I usually feel its incomparable power flooding my whole body, often resulting in delightful tingling sensations especially in my hands. It's as though my inner Light body and grid's dimmer switch gets turned up, even reaching the metaphorical equivalent of 300W power brilliance and intensity.

This deceptively simple yet priceless tool, when used with pure intent, has the added benefit of ensuring your I AM Power flow stays fully activated. You can also use it at any time when you are faced with challenging energies or feel "out of tune."

Divine I AM Decree. Another excellent tool I've been using almost daily since the '80s that helps maintain my Higher Power focus and energy is the I AM Decree. It superbly encapsulates a wealth of information about who you truly are and your divinity.

Don't be fooled by its deceptive simplicity, though. Provided you think about each phrase slowly, the more you use it the more insights arise that expand your understanding. If you are saying it as rote without thinking, you might just as well be saying, *Baa baa black sheep!* Here it is:

Divine I AM Decree

I AM
I am all that I AM
I AM one with the Infinite Mind
I AM one with the Source of all life
I AM one with all life forms and they are one with me
I AM Love
I AM Light
I AM Peace
I AM

Notice how this decree succinctly reaffirms all the main principles intrinsic to I AM mastery we've already explored. *I am all that I AM*—notice how the personality *I am* becomes your Higher Self *I AM*, referring to your limitless potential as a creation of divine Love and Light. Being one with the Infinite Mind means that whatever you can conceive is already part of the Universal Intelligence and therefore possible.

Remembering you are one with the source of all life confirms that as your birthright you can access the Power without limit to bring into expression in whatever form you choose, effortlessly and perfectly. As we all remember, we are one with all life forms, so our resolve to live and work co-operatively as members of *Team Humanity* is strengthened, along with how we treat all creatures and our Mother Earth.

I AM Love makes a powerful statement about your real Self. As I say it, I often add extensions such as, *I AM loving, forgiving and forgiven, lovable and much loved.*

I AM Light reminds you that because your mind is part of the Divine Mind, you can receive illumination and inspiration at all times, and have light thrown onto whatever you don't understand.

I AM Peace indicates that through putting your I AM in charge, you can be free of fear and develop absolute trust, the requirement for inner peace of mind.

Then you can add the following invocation if it's relevant for you. It is a perfect way of affirming precisely what level you intend to communicate with and ensures you keep free of lower psychic interference:

Invocation of Intention and Protection

By the Power of that which I AM,
I invoke only the Light from the Masters
and Teachers of the Higher Mental and Spiritual planes
and beyond.
And I refuse all communication that
originates on the astral plane
or is not working in the Light of God
and with the Divine Plan.
I AM

The Miraculous *Aha*

It's always an exhilarating experience when you have an *Aha* moment. Suddenly, you know the perfect answer to an important question or what decision to make, or the best action to take pops into your head. Often a solution defies any logical reasoning, but deep down you know it's the most perfect solution possible. On occasion, you may have thought about it too much and then decided to go the logical way, especially if you have to explain it to someone else. Inevitably, you realize too late that the original inspiration would have been best, but at least you learned something from it.

When you do follow the *Aha* moment, however, the sense of satisfaction from its rightness is a wonderful and precious experience. But instead of relying only on random flashes, wouldn't it be better to get those right *Aha* moments on demand?

Yes, it is possible. When you are faced with wanting any kind of inspiration, my technique is simple—you guessed it—ask HS. The reason HS's solutions are far better than anything you can figure out yourself is because your HS has an overview of the bigger picture, whereas on the earth plane you can only see what is around you from your limited vision and understanding. In addition, your I AM Higher Self only has your best interests at heart and knows what is perfect for you in any situation or time.

To ask for guidance or inspiration I say something like: *HS, please bring into my conscious awareness the inspiration (or guidance) I require for_____.*

Super Suggestions

Here are a few more energy maintenance suggestions to keep your inner and outer worlds in harmony:

- To maintain your acquaintance with your HS, feel its peace within and surrounding you as often as possible. Always remember your HS does not judge, compare, or demand that you be better than anyone else.

- In any situation, remember you can go beyond the restriction of the physical plane by asking your Higher Self for assistance to create the life you desire.

- In your inner heart-Soul sanctuary, aim to let go of all attachments that rely on the external world of the ego. This allows your HS power into the physical plane to help you.

- Remember that your HS not only has a bird's eye view of your life and desires that are the very best for you, but can transcend the usual limited horizontal view. Think of the sacred symbol of the even-sided cross which represents the bringing down of spirit into matter: +

- Surrender and trust in the invincible power, energy, perfection, and intelligence you have at your disposal. (Remember my *PEOPLISM* anagram—Chapter 3.) Such allowing and trust is not only your cornerstone of real freedom, it's the secret of miracles.

CHAPTER 12

Master Secret #3: Focus on Your Perfect Outcome

We've all met sincere folk—maybe you're one yourself—who dearly want to discover the secret of manifestation. They say things like, *I've read the right books, tried the Law of Attraction, understand the theories—but exactly **how** can I make it work in my life? Are there any precise instructions I can follow that guarantee success?*

The answer is a resounding *yes*! And you've already made a good start with the necessary preparations outlined in Steps I and II of this guidebook. You've changed your limited mindset and restored your I AM Source Power connection and flow. You've cleared what's been stopping you up until now, and all your power switches are turned to "on." Now you are ready to learn the master secret that will activate the practical applications and subsequent techniques you will read about in Step IV.

My I AM HS gave me this fail-safe master secret that answers the perennial question of *how* to manifest anything you desire for a life of Heaven on Earth. It is simply this:

Keep your focus only on the perfect outcome. Then hand it over to your Higher Self to fulfill.

Leave all details of how, by what means, through whom to HS, your source of Divine Authority and unfailing power. In other words, don't sweat the small stuff!

You can so easily get bogged down with all the details of manifesting what you want, worried that you'll forget certain important parts, or trying to figure out how to manifest your deepest desires in precisely the right way. The result more often than not is—*zilch*.

So why can you be certain of a perfect outcome? Divine thoughts can only be of perfection. All you have to do is allow them to express through you and then sit back and enjoy the miracles. By being willing to allow your I AM HS to be in charge, you're letting go of the need for your limited, small ego self to stay in the driver's seat. This is a great blessing and means no more hit-and-miss results or "hoping for the best."

The only point to remember is this: having decreed the outcome that's seemingly perfect at this moment, relax and quit wondering or even thinking about its progress or how it will come into physical form. And most importantly, release all attachment to it manifesting exactly as your mind conceives. Allow it to be divinely perfect. This ensures the outcome will always be sublimely wonderful and often more perfect than you even envisioned.

So, just hold the finished perfection firmly in your consciousness as having already manifested, and imprint it on the Quantum Field. It's as simple as that— and you don't need to keep repeating time-consuming affirmations. This superb master secret is summarized in the 3 easy steps below:

3-Step Fail-Safe "Perfect Outcome" Technique

1. ***Simply state your perfect outcome as the whole finished picture.*** Word it as succinctly as possible, both in your mind and in a written form. And always include the magic word, *perfect* or *perfectly*. This encompasses every single aspect, every tiny detail, so you don't have to list them individually. It also means you don't need to worry about forgetting something important.

To me, *perfect* is truly a magical word that ensures not only a successful outcome I'm envisioning right now, but allows HS to add wonderful extras I hadn't even dreamed of. This has happened time and time again. You'll love how your outcomes are more perfectly marvelous in ways beyond your wildest imagination.

2. ***Once you've stated your perfect outcome, hand it over to HS to fulfill.*** You can say, *HS, you take care of it please.* Think of a restaurant order: you don't tell the chef what ingredients to use and how to cook them. You simply order the dish of your choice, confident that all the details will be taken care of and that it will be delivered just as you expected.

3. ***Imprint what the completed perfect outcome looks and feels like, in the Quantum Field.*** See what your new situation looks like as an already accomplished fact in the Quantum Source Field. Your mind, guided and powered by your Higher Self Mind, is part of this field. Doing this provides a blueprint upon which you then focus your attention and thoughts as a "done deal," wholly and perfectly recorded.

The energy and high vibrational frequency this creates magnetizes all the necessary support, synchronicities, and serendipities to you, far beyond what your physical self could ever accomplish. Quite often, this superior result occurs through what appears to be divine orchestration.

> Then, all you have to do is maintain your conscious observation—what science calls the *observer effect*—until your outcome is replicated in physical form. The importance of observation is that you're not projecting some unfulfilled desire in the future. You are manifesting in the present what has already been created in the field of limitless potential. Herein lies the secret key to success.

Sounds so simple, doesn't it? And it is, but not necessarily so easy to accept at first glance. It took me a while to really understand the brilliance and effortless efficacy of this master key of manifestation. But I am a "spiritual technician" and so I've investigated and tested this and all the techniques I share, to prove beyond doubt that they work perfectly every time. Be patient with yourself. Let your success be your proof and joy.

The beauty and remarkable rapid effectiveness of this fail-safe technique is that by going directly to the highest aspect of your Divine Self, you bypass anything lower or in between. The axiatonal lines restoration process you learned in Chapter 10 helps this enormously. You don't have to rely on a third party as in channeling—that would be a contradiction in terms. Instead, you awaken your own dormant power and unleash your birthright of incredible potential.

The perfect simplicity of this master secret may cause a response of *But* ..... or *What if* ..... We are so used to having to *do* things ourselves with no other help, that a period of conscious application and perseverance may be necessary for you to fully take this new concept on board. Use the technique with an open mind and prove for yourself that it works. It may help to go back and re-read Step I to help you get more familiar and comfortable with the underlying principles of the real you who has this power.

The Quantum Source Field

The Quantum Source Field is the field of all potential, an aspect of the Divine Infinite Mind or Universal Intelligence where creation begins and is maintained as a Divine thought. It contains all knowledge, information and limitless possibilities. Think about that a moment. There is nothing that isn't potentially possible within the Quantum Source Field.

Even though it's far beyond what your finite human mind can grasp, this field of Divine Consciousness responds to you because of who you really are. This Intelligence records your serious intentions carefully, especially your fearless decrees. It then creates forms that exactly match your focus, your thoughts, and your feelings about them. Imagine that. It's as if the Quantum Source Field is saying, *Your wish is my command.*

Your job is simply to observe the finished product that you've consciously created and recorded in partnership with your HS, and bring it down into the material plane.

Another benefit of tapping into the Quantum Source Field is once you have imprinted all you've learned so far in the Field, it becomes easier to quickly remember it should you temporarily become distracted. Make the decree to do so, for example, *With the restored Power of my Higher God-Self, I AM imprinting all my Miracle-Effect knowledge in the Quantum Field.*

Sylvia Vowless, QSM

The Magic in Welcoming Change

For many, the idea of change is a scary thought, especially for those who have always wanted to be in charge of their life and outcomes. You have the option when formulating your perfect outcome, of controlling the result by focusing only on steps you see as leading to a final goal. No doubt this is what you are used to doing, so if this feels more comfortable to you, then by all means continue to use this approach. However, I've found that going straight to my ultimate outcome is far more magical and seems to allow even more miracles to support me along the way. But to use this method, you have to be unfazed by any changes in your life that may need to occur.

For example, let's say you decide to leave your safe and secure job because it's not satisfying you any longer. You can specify your outcome as the usual next logical step by including the type of work, the salary range, location and so on you desire. Or you can allow your HS to work miracles by simply stating that you require and/or desire your next most perfect occupation or step to manifest. This takes courage but could result in the most exciting and amazing change of life and work direction that would probably have never entered your mind. Without doubt, it would involve change in many ways, so be certain you feel okay with that possibility.

Many people regard change as something unpleasant or to be feared, and yet we're quite happy with positive changes on a daily basis. Think of the weather, the seasons, personal progress, and so on. I was in the former category back in 1990 when I met Eileen Caddy in her caravan at the thriving Findhorn community in Scotland that she founded through her higher guidance. We spent a delightful morning together comparing our service work and philosophies, discovering that we both taught the three Ps of Perseverance/Persistence, Patience and Peace.

However, she made a throw-away remark which has stuck in my mind ever since. She said, "I welcome change." I remember her words sent shivers up my spine. At that time, this was a challenging even scary thought, because I was still working through my major leap of faith in giving up everything connected to my life routine and previous security. *I'm certainly not ready to welcome any more changes,* I thought to myself.

Little did I know then, that that year's adventure would be the first of many changes challenging my comfort zone. My way of life and sense of security until then had been defined by having a home and normal life routine. But now I too, can enthusiastically say, *I welcome change.* I'm excited at what my Higher Self knows I'm ready to tackle next, even though I never have any idea until it unfolds. This is why, when I finish any particular project or stage in my Soul Service, I say to HS, *Please reveal to my conscious mind my next most perfect step.*

Miracles Not Created Consciously

So far you've been learning how you can *consciously* create miracles by being clear on various perfect outcomes and letting go of all attachment as to how they will occur.

I've discovered, however, that there are other kinds of miracles besides those so far discussed. There are unexpected or *surprise* miracles, and those that occur through *divine orchestration* and also through *divine intervention*. All, however, rest on the same foundation of holding, without faltering, a *miracle consciousness* which is the result of integrating and applying what you've learned so far. This creates the essential environment for miracles of any kind to occur, including surprise miracles that seem to just happen without any conscious focus on your part.

Surprise Miracles

When a miracle occurs without any thought or intention on our part, I believe it is our soul and HS intervening on our behalf.

A surprise miracle happened to me back in 1963 when I survived against all odds, what would have normally been a fatal car accident. I clearly remember the first words I heard from some who saw it happen and wanting to help, rushed to my upturned car where I was trapped: "My God, it's a miracle someone is still alive in there!" I realized some years later the reason for this miracle was that my soul had to find a way to stop me spending this lifetime on a path that wasn't part of my Higher Self chosen purpose for incarnating now.

Before this life-changing event, I'd had a few soul nudges trying to get my attention, but I paid them no heed. After all, I was following my passion for teaching dancing, even though after eight years, a feeling of "divine discontent" had begun to stir within me. I ignored these signs and so attracted what in retrospect I see was a cosmic four-by-two!

The only way to stop me in my tracks long enough to get me to turn within and evaluate my life was something as drastic as breaking my back. It certainly worked very effectively. Lying in hospital while the spinal graft healed gave me months of enforced reflection time. As a consequence, I later broke off my engagement which hadn't been right for either of us. But being stubborn, it took me another year before I was ready to give up my ballet studios and move on.

Divine Orchestration

Miracles of the third kind are those that manifest in the form of what appears to be a divine orchestration of events or connections. Divine orchestration miracles are seemingly chance meetings or synchronicities whose outcome or answer is far beyond what you would normally expect or even think possible.

For example, before attending an event recently where I knew no one, I had decreed the perfect outcome that I would be led to the perfect person crucial for completing this book. Just before the event was to start, I received an intuitive impulse to go into the restroom—and not for the usual reason. There happened to be only one other person in there, so I struck up a conversation with this charming lady with whom I immediately felt a connection. I discovered that from among the over 550 people attending the event, this special lady was exactly the right person to fulfill my requirements in every possible way. It's such a blessing working with this higher knowledge and power that is available to all.

In 2005, an entirely different kind of experience occurred. The previous year after I returned home from yet another demanding world teaching and speaking tour, I made a definite choice that I stated to HS in no uncertain terms. I decided I wasn't going to do any more big trips as part of my Soul Service. I said that Australia was as far as I ever wanted to go because travelling alone around the world to European and Scandinavian countries year after year was getting too exhausting and physically demanding. I was well into my sixties by then, and it's not easy being a woman travelling on her own, as well as trusting everything would be fine in each new and unknown place I'd been invited.

However, the following April, I received an email from an organization in Turkey I'd never heard of, inviting me to be one of four international speakers that included Dr Eric Pearl, founder of the energy healing process known as Reconnective Healing, at their annual *Call to World Peace and Unity* symposium in November. I immediately assumed they didn't realize I live down under in New Zealand, as travel that far is very expensive from here. I felt honored of course, but I didn't respond right away because I had a friend visiting. A day later the phone rang. It was from Turkey asking if I'd received their email and reiterating that they would very much like me to come and be a speaker.

Apparently two people connected with the symposium had recommended me, one from America and the other from Israel. They both knew of my work and had heard me speak before. The Turkish folks did realize I was in New Zealand, and they particularly wanted me as I was the first person they'd invited as a "spiritual ambassador" from the southern hemisphere. Flustered, I made all the excuses I could think of to decline, as the thought of travelling that far for five days to give a half hour paper just didn't appeal. Finally I explained how the long hours sitting in cramped seats in a plane was not only tiring but not good for my grafted spine.

"No problem," was the answer, "We'll book you in business class so you can stretch out and be comfortable, and you'll have a night's stay over at Dubai to rest and break the long journey both ways."

What could I say to that? At this point, I realized that for some reason HS wanted me to go, so reluctantly I agreed. In retrospect, apart from being privileged to contribute to an amazing and valuable global event, I understood there were two other important personal reasons I was being set up to go.

The main one was to encourage me to change my stance about international travel in the future. Had I stuck to stubbornly refusing even to consider invitations to speak and teach in Scandinavia and Europe, the miracle-defining experience of 2006 that changed the direction of my life could not have occurred. And the subsequent years of experimenting with creating miracles that has led me to living the Miracle Effect that I'm now sharing with you might never have happened. Fortunately, I got over myself and since then have travelled globally again when invited as part of my Soul Service work.

The other very personal reason was to understand more about the early Sufi form of Islam. I still carried a couple of horrific recalls of past life suffering at the hands of militant interpretations that I hadn't completely resolved and released. Of course, the beautiful people in the organization were all Sufi Muslims working for world peace. They explained the tenets of Islam, which gave me an expanded knowledge of this gentle religion based upon love, brotherhood, and unity. It was an unforgettable experience which I shall always treasure.

Divine Intervention

The fourth kind of miracle acts like a hugely comforting safety-net principle that has proved invaluable to me on several occasions. If you've put your Higher Self in charge of your life, you are in effect giving permission for divine intervention via the Holy Spirit to happen if or when it's in your best interest. For example, should you inadvertently start focusing on an outcome that's not for your own or others' highest good and happiness, or is not in the best timing, this kind of miracle is truly a God-send.

To show you how divine intervention works, read about a recent chain of events I experienced (I'm still chuckling at myself for getting to the point of such a miracle being necessary).

My right knee first started acting up very painfully in 1988, then more severely in the mid-1990's. After more than 40 years teaching dancing, it was worn out. The specialist told me that he couldn't do anything then but advised me to come back in 15 or more years' time when he was sure there would be a surgical procedure to fix it. I didn't have higher understandings back then, so I accepted this as the answer, which was dutifully recorded in my subconscious mind. Since then, I've had bouts of discomfort that, until recent years, I've managed to get through.

However, after being told at my clinic check-ups over the past six years that x-rays showed a knee replacement was required, this year I agreed to the surgery without questioning. A minor incident had caused my knee to become rather annoyingly uncomfortable, so with the subconscious program of "they can fix it" running, I agreed to be scheduled for surgery. A few weeks later, the day of the operation arrived, and everything was prepared—dog in kennel, dinners in the freezer, and so on. I arrived at the hospital and after the final checks, I got all gowned, soxed and hatted up, ready to be taken into the operating theatre by the surgeon.

This is when the divine intervention occurred. A different surgeon, who was vastly more aware than the one I'd previously been seeing, came in to introduce himself and take me through to the operating theatre next door.

After questioning me and looking rather quizzical at my answers, he finally asked me if I was sure I wanted to have the surgery. To say I was flabbergasted is an understatement. Completely confused, I didn't know what to think or say, except what I was told appeared to be the case on x-ray. But what came next, his profound comment of "I don't treat an x-ray. I treat the whole person," acted as a reality check that helped me put it all in perspective.

The surgeon gave me time to gather my thoughts while he did the next operation. After asking for HS help and clarity, I found myself wondering what on earth I was doing there. After all, I'd already self-healed two congenital degenerative bone conditions that were considered medically untreatable. But while I still had the "surgeon will fix it" program for my knee running unconsciously, I wouldn't be able to self-heal.

All this became crystal clear during my hour or so of inner questioning. I realized that I could heal the knee pain myself as soon as I deleted the unconscious program that someone else could do it. I literally skipped out of the hospital, relieved I'd escaped major surgery that I've since heard may not have even helped, or worse still, might have left me with permanent pain.

Since then, I've been applying the appropriate techniques for my self-healing, so I can live and move easily and eventually pain-free. Another bonus of living the Miracle Effect is that the more you work with your Higher Power, the quicker you enjoy success.

If you are wondering how to give your HS permission to intervene on your behalf, then simply hold that intention and start your decrees with *I AM* ... or *Through the Power of my I AM Higher Self* ... By putting them under this higher authority, you are automatically giving permission.

Food for Thought

Something I've discovered time and time again is that miracles often manifest at the eleventh hour—or in the case of my recent hospital escape, at the eleven-and-three-quarters hour. I've frequently wondered why this is so. One thought so far is that since miracles are always above and beyond normal manifestations, we have to allow the space for them to come into the earth's frequency range. As soon as we panic or begin to have doubts, we close the door.

I also wonder if the 11th hour phenomenon is a necessary part of the Miracle Effect training. In other words, to become a divine expression in human form, you have to develop absolute trust and certainty in your Higher Power. As with all success training, if it came too easily, we would never reach our highest potential.

CHAPTER 13
Master Secret #4: Tool-Box Essentials

Emergency MIND CPR

One of the many tools my HS has given me is a brilliantly effective technique I call *Emergency MIND CPR* because it can metaphorically save your life as you develop the Miracle Effect. So what makes this one necessary to know and use?

As human beings, we all have what Eastern sages call a *monkey mind*. The estimated 30 to 50 thousand thoughts that pass through your mind each day run you around like disruptive monkeys playing tricks and wasting time. How often have you thought, for example, *I hope such and such doesn't happen,* or *I'll never have...*? I'm sure you can think of many instances.

Never fear, help is here! This unfocussed state is part of the "normal" human condition, but as you begin to integrate higher consciousness into your life, you can catch your monkey mind more quickly and more often before it does any real mischief. However, being human, unwanted thoughts from time to time will still pop into your mind, or unwanted words can come out of your mouth before you can stop them, so here's my perfect solution: Apply Emergency MIND CPR!

Emergency MIND CPR Technique

<u>C</u> - The minute you catch a negative or disempowering thought scampering across your mind—or a doubt expressed by thought or words—about successfully manifesting your desired perfect outcome, immediately say firmly to yourself or more specifically, to your subconscious mind: *Cancel, Cancel, Cancel!*

If you notice any lingering energy or emotional charge around your thought or words then you can repeat *Cancel* as often as you feel is necessary. The aim is to know you have taken conscious control and stopped any possible destructive effect. If you cannot say *Cancel* aloud, then saying it under your breath or even mentally still works.

<u>P</u> - Promptly create a concise **positive phrase** that expresses the polar opposite of the disempowering thought and *only* the perfect outcome you do want. This is the *Universal Law of the Word* in action, a law that explains how thoughts are unspoken words carrying creative power. There's a very apt colloquial saying that goes: *Name it and it's yours.* For fun, you could think of wording your desired outcome so that your Fairy Godmother, were she to hear it, would know exactly what to give you!

<u>R</u> - **Repeat** your positive phrase often, saying it with conviction and absolute certainty, preferably saying it aloud to imprint it firmly in both your conscious and unconscious minds. Known as *habituation*, this is a powerful way to get your subconscious mind to record the new outcome, so it becomes permanently fixed. Remember how you learned your multiplication times tables or how you automatically drive a car without having to think of each action? Same thing here.

This then replaces the cancelled, unwanted thought with the perfect outcome you desire, an essential step to ensure a void is not left that could get filled with similar, destructive thoughts. You are applying another universal law, the *Law of Reversal*. Notice how powerfully these laws affect every part of living with awareness.

To finish this technique, see yourself in your mind already enjoying the outcome. The more emotion or energy in motion you can add, the better.

This technique fits with the recent scientific understanding of the *neuro-plasticity* of the brain, which says that the brain's pathways are not permanent, they can be altered. In other words, you can release debilitating thoughts and memories, and develop new ways of thinking and perceiving the world, so you don't have to stay with your old fixed viewpoints.

Ongoing Action

As just mentioned, it's essential that you continually check and become more aware of your habitual thought patterns. If you catch yourself thinking—even fleetingly—about anything less than the outcome you desire, immediately apply Emergency Mind CPR. Recall the third Vibrational Law that states we have to apply a higher vibrational frequency—in this case, positive thoughts about your perfect outcome manifesting—to make a permanent change. Otherwise, your lower frequency doubts will reign supreme and sabotage your success.

Similarly, continually check your vibrational frequency by noticing how you are feeling and how your body is behaving. Find the cause and apply Emergency Mind CPR.

Pablo Picasso once remarked that action is the key to all success.

The more you do these simple self-checks, the easier you'll find it becomes to stay on track and focussed. Your Miracle Me Self becomes more and more the natural *you,* and the enjoyment and quality of your life will reflect this. You may find that whenever anyone asks how you are, instead of the usual response of *good, fine* or *OK,* you automatically give an enthusiastic response reflecting your deep sense of *joie de vivre.* When I do this, not only do I feel even more upbeat, but I've noticed how this response registers with the other person, often resulting in a big smile—a win-win action.

Be Here Now

You can only create by focusing your thoughts in the "now" moment. I find this saying sums up an extremely important truth: *The past is history, the future a mystery, only today contains the present.* I translate this in my life as looking back on past experiences only in order to see the lessons in them as gifts of insights and understanding I needed to recognize at the time—and to give thanks for how far I've come. The lessons learned strengthen and expand my foundation, and are a necessary preparation for launching higher and higher aims.

Learn from the past, but then let it go. The past cannot be undone or changed. Allow any failures, misfortunes, or mistakes you made to guide and equip you for a greater experience of life. Never be tempted to use them as excuses for staying stuck, for inaction, for holding you back, or for believing you are unable to create the life of your dreams. Excuses be gone!

Challenges come and go. The only constant is your ability to choose how you respond each time. And each of these times is a defining moment. The external world of circumstances only controls and limits you if you allow it to. It's your internal world, the stuff of the real Miracle Me that's within to guide you towards becoming all you can be—and enjoy life to the fullest extent possible.

Now is the only time it's possible to create the life you long to live. Not in remembering the past, not in projecting into the future, but now. Progress comes from living each day with mindfulness and ever-expanding awareness. The eternal now is the precious gift of life given to us moment by moment. Therefore, only recall your past with gratitude. Hold on to the lessons, the understandings gained from each experience or challenge, that have brought you right here to this present minute.

And most of all, remember your joys, your ups rather than downs, your successes and achievements, great and small. Acknowledge them all. Smile at the past, celebrate each *now* moment, and excitedly create the future you would love to live.

If you ever doubted your self-worth or felt not good enough, look at how you've managed to weather all of life's storms well enough to be able to recognize you are master of your life and future, right now. Accept that you are powerful and knowledgeable enough to create the life of your dreams. Hold on to your vision of what you choose and desire in your life becoming your reality. *Go for it!*

Taking Time Out

The frenetic lifestyle that most people succumb to leaves little time for anything beyond just managing to exist. But if you're reading this book, you must have come to the realization that there is more to life than this "mouse-on-a-treadmill" existence. The only way to get balance back is to take regular time out.

However you like to do this doesn't matter, as long as it includes precious *me time* when you allow yourself to dream and focus your thoughts to design whatever perfect outcomes you can envision. Equally, reflecting regularly upon the tools and techniques that you're learning and how better to apply them, is the complementary key to your success.

Contemplation

I make contemplation part of every morning. My reflection time includes bringing to mind and giving thanks for all the facets that make my life so wonderful, the beauty all around me, and the music I love that fills my home. I think about the way I intend my day to unfold. I invite and allow inspiration and ideas from HS to come into my conscious awareness. This is an essential part of my life, a pro-active component of developing a Miracle Effect way of living.

Do you find it difficult to relax, unwind and switch off your constant stream of thoughts and self-talk, let alone contemplate? Here's something I discovered that helped me to develop my contemplation ability. In 1963 I found myself forced to lie flat in a hospital bed for four long, tedious, seemingly endless months, able only to move my arms. Before the accident, I had just started back teaching my ballet studio classes after the summer holidays with all the anticipation and excitement a new year brings, and to be so bed-ridden seemed like hell on earth. As well as being in shock and pain from the car accident and resulting broken back, I felt incredibly resentful and trapped.

Eventually, I came to realize the only way through this major crisis was to find activities that would help me let go of the tension and make life a little more tolerable. I learned to contemplate. It was the only way I could switch my mind off from dwelling on the tedium of each interminably long day. There was no television back then and visiting hours were strictly limited.

I found the answer was to focus deeply on a single flower. I would hold the flower close and study every tiny detail, including its delicate yet intense color, variations in hue, translucence and petal shapes, texture, and exquisitely intricate formation. I'd observe buds opening imperceptibly over a period of time. Iceland Poppies were especially fascinating from the time they popped their hairy caps to gradually smoothing out their tightly crinkled petals to reveal their full beauty.

You might find a similar technique works in helping you to relax, unwind, and develop a worthwhile contemplation practice. Any single flower will do; it doesn't matter whether it's a rose or a daisy picked from a grassy area. Each and every one is beauty and perfection made manifest.

Are You Listening?

If you only allow time for talking—whether decreeing, praying or chanting—then how will you ever be able to hear the supreme guidance from Holy Spirit to smooth your life journey? How can divine inspiration or solutions reach your awareness? It's like talking on the phone and not pausing to hear the other person's replies.

Only by giving yourself the gift of regular periods of contemplation and meditation—if not every day, then as often as possible—can you make the best use of this incarnation. It doesn't have to involve hours. Frequent, short periods can be extraordinarily valuable, as long as you're able to relax, be still and silent as you switch off from everyday concerns, knowing you won't be disturbed. (Note that the same letters spell out both words: *silent* and *listen*.)

Relaxing music helps many people, or chanting a mantra helps others to "tune in." Find what works best for you and what time of the day gets the best results. I read recently that research in neuroscience shows "night owls" are more inwardly productive in the morning, and for "larks," it's the evening. Although this doesn't seem to make sense at first glance, think about it: you accomplish the most successful physical and practical activity through using left brain intellect and logic at night if you are an owl, or in the morning, if a lark. However, your best inner HS inspiration, intuitive results, and guidance come at the *less* mentally and physically active part of the day when your right brain can be more active. I had already found this out for myself, since being a night owl, I give myself time most mornings to tune in through contemplation and meditation. I've also found that I usually get the most inspiration and clarity lying down, something else that was reported. Strange but true.

Meditation Benefits

In addition to contemplation, another life-enhancing practice is meditation. The gifts this regular "time out" habit gives are too numerous to list here, but with so much research available showing the benefits in physical, psychological and spiritual wellbeing, there's no longer any room for doubt.

I proved this for myself in 1979 when, having read over and over that meditation was a necessary step for spiritual progress, I began meditating daily in earnest. Deep insights and understandings soon followed, continuing to this day.

An important note here: Don't beat yourself up if you miss a day or three every so often. The good news is that the beneficial effects of regular meditation are cumulative. Even if your vibrational frequency does drop, the base line is much higher than when you first started, so the effect is less noticeable. And you won't suffer any permanent set-back.

CHAPTER 14
Success Secrets Summary

Why does success seem to happen more effortlessly and perfectly for some people than for others? It depends upon how deeply you have integrated and actively apply the numerous key points we've covered so far into your everyday living. In this chapter I've added a few self-check reminders, plus some extra tips to help you.

Self-Check and Tips

Ask yourself how conscious you are now of the following master points for living the Miracle Effect:

- You have as your reality the necessary awareness of who your real Self is, partnered with total acceptance of your higher potential (detailed in Step I).
- You understand how to raise your vibrations and maintain them at high enough levels for I AM mastery on a day-to-day basis.
- You have created an unrestricted HS connection through clearing blocks and limitations in whatever form were relevant for you.
- You are regularly taking effective action by living from the place of power I call your Miracle Me, by mastering your lower self, then developing and living the Miracle Effect. I find it extremely valuable to ask myself often, *Who's in charge, anyway?* This simple question reminds me at which level I'm

choosing to work from—third dimensional "little me" or fifth dimensional HS.

• You remember to get out of your own way. Doubts and thinking *it's too good to be true* cause tension. Tension restricts flow and acts like an instant mind switch, figuratively turning the power off.

An instant antidote is to remember to smile and relax. How? Try holding a pen or pencil in your teeth! This puts your mouth into a smiling position. A wonderful thing then happens. Your brain doesn't distinguish between you smiling because you're actually happy or just making the movement. It simply reacts by releasing feel-good endorphins. These not only help you release tension but also help reduce any aches or pains you may have. And if you look at yourself in the mirror, guess what? You'll certainly be smiling for real.

Reminder Cue Cards for Success Checks

A simple idea I find invaluable for helping me keep my heavenly focus is making small cue cards. You'd no doubt find this a very useful little tool, too. Write key thoughts or reminders on small cards, preferably with colored pens or felt-tips. I buy the place-name cards that fold in half and stand on their own. Carry them with you or put them where you'll see them many times throughout each day. I always have a couple on my coffee table and fridge that I change from time to time, depending upon my current focus.

Cue cards can also help maintain high vibrational thoughts and emotional frequencies, especially when handling the stresses of today's life. Here are several suggestions that perfectly summarize key points and may inspire you. Choose those that resonate or create your own wording. *(Note:* I use the words *require* and *desire*, never the word *need* because it's a loaded word, based on fear and anxiety and so is unlikely to be fulfilled. Also, I never use the word *want*. *Want* has ongoing connotations of lack and being left still wanting. *Desire* is a far preferable word to use in its place, as well as having a much greater punch.

> *My unfailing I AM is:*
> **I – Invincible, A – All-Power and Perfection, M – Miracle Me Manifesting!**

I find this simple truism helps strengthen and maintain my Miracle-Effect and reminds me of Jesus' enormously powerful statement: *Of myself I can do nothing; it is the God-Self in me that does the work.* (In the scriptures, the generic term used for the God-Self was *Father*.)

> **R + D = SO — Require + Deserve = Successful Outcomes.**

If you feel deep down that you don't really deserve the best life has to offer, then your requirements aren't likely to be met in a satisfying, abundant way. Reset your self-image before going any further. Remember to say every day with conviction the Divine I AM Decree, taking particular note of your two selves (your personality self *I am* and your *Higher Self I AM*) in: *I am all that I AM.*

> **D + L = SO — Desire + Limitlessness = Successful Outcomes.**

Again, if you believe in lack rather than the truth that the universe and creation are limitless, no matter what you do, your desires are likely to remain unfulfilled. If you happen to be a Star Trek fan you could instead use the captain's famous punchline: *Make it so.*

My God-Effect C I A Formula – Conceive Completion
with Certainty + **I AM** Intention = Actualize/Achieve

This useful cue card can strengthen your perseverance and help you maintain the necessary relaxed state of mind.

Important Questions

When I teach my Miracle Me workshop, I invite questions to ensure that the information is meaningful to everyone. Here are some that most frequently arise:

- One of the most often asked queries is how other people figure in your perfect outcomes. The answer rests on the basic premise that you are co-creating with your personal Higher Self Power. As every person has this same ability, you cannot interfere with another's desires or their free will. You cannot force them into your picture. However, if two or more people's outcomes have complementary intention of similar vibrational frequencies, then the *Law of Attraction* may bring you together, bearing in mind there may be karmic factors involved as well.

- Another important consideration is the influence of the *Law of Detachment*. If you are rigidly or emotionally attached to the outcome occurring exactly as you envision or with only one special person, then you're doing three things. First, your emotional involvement creates tension because you've put your lower self in the driver's seat. Second, from this lower vantage point, you short-circuit any possible input of your Higher Self's power and perfection—and miracles. Third and most importantly, you prevent the divine intervention safety-net that can save you from a less than perfect or happy outcome manifesting if required.

• No doubt you have many outcomes in mind that you'd like to manifest. Recall the truism that energy goes where your focus stays. This means that until you become highly efficient at manifesting, it's best to focus only on the one outcome immediately at hand or the most pressing one. Once you see signs of success—or better still, complete your success—then focus on another.

This may be a good point to pause and formulate an outcome dear to your heart right now. I suggest you start with a modest goal to build your trust and confidence. Then, once you have transformed belief into real knowing, free of even the tiniest doubt that this HS methodology really does deliver, you are ready to move on to focusing on major outcomes. You can word it something like: *With my fully active Higher Self power, I decree that the perfect outcome of _____ manifests effortlessly in the perfect way and in the perfect time. I give thanks that it is so.*

More 3-Ps Power Switches

All is not what it appears to be. You are conditioned to think that outer appearances are the only reality. Yet you actually live in two worlds. These two worlds, the inner and outer, the seen and the unseen, is where you co-exist simultaneously at all times. As soon as you begin to co-ordinate the two, amazing things can happen.

Having journeyed with me thus far, you already know how your unseen or inner reality can manifest into the seen or outer third dimension reality through your conscious direction. Here are two suggestions that make good cue cards to help remind you of this:

Higher Self Inner Three Ps. Never forget that HS is your unfailing source of the fifth dimensional qualities of *Power*, *Plenty* and *Perfection*. The more consistently you keep your focus on these three Ps, the more you keep your power switch in the "on" position. If you forget, and try to work from a lower level, then everything grinds to a halt, especially effortless manifestation.

Perfection is infinite, forever expanding and evolving. What was perfect for you a year or ten years ago isn't your current ideal today. What today is perfect for you right now may not seem perfect tomorrow. Yet because of the limiting third-dimensional boxes we are so used to living in, we think of perfection as being finite, static and unchangeable.

Allow your perceptions to keep expanding. Working from your HS fifth-dimensional perspective causes all limitations to fall away. Nothing has to stay the same. Enjoying ongoing new expressions and new levels of perfection that include more marvelous aspects than you're able to envision in this moment is the fantastic result. The same principle applies to living Heaven on Earth as a Miracle Me. The sky—or your highest potential—really has no limit.

Three Ps of Attitude and Thought. Hand in hand with the Higher Self "on" switches are three that are under your conscious control: *Purpose* with *Persistence* or determination, and *Patience*.

We've talked about clarity of purpose in knowing exactly how to frame your outcomes. But until you become a Manifestation Master, some goals may take time to come into form, hence the reminder about staying certain and relaxed, and especially being patient.

Persistence also implies willingness to persevere. How willing are you? What's on your "unwilling list?" If you find yourself thinking things like, *I haven't enough time or energy ... I'm too busy ... There's too much to think about or do ...* then pause and consider what beliefs or emotions are behind those thoughts. Whatever they are—feeling you don't deserve an extraordinary life, that you're not special or clever enough to succeed, for example—are ego-tricks. Acknowledge any such disempowering beliefs and then delete them from your consciousness. Re-reading Step I to reassure yourself of the truth of who you are will help to renew your enthusiasm and certainty.

Your I AM Limitless Power can then pour through you to manifest into whatever form or expression you desire—effortlessly, joyfully, perfectly and with comfort and ease. Remember the *Law of Commitment* quote from Chapter 5. When you add time, energy, and desire, then you're a certain winner.

Your Next Step ...

In Step III, you unlocked the secrets of success for becoming empowered to live Heaven on Earth every day. In Step IV we get down to the *nitty gritty* of actually designing your exciting personal journey of creating Heaven on Earth, using my tried and true practical ways.

STEP IV:

Design Your Life to Live Heaven on Earth

CHAPTER 15
THE Big Question

Back in the mid-1960s when I first seriously started looking into spirituality, I purchased a home study course of ancient wisdom. Towards the bottom of the very first page, I read: *What do you want?* The question was accompanied by the directive not to turn to the next page until you had answered the question.

I puzzled over that question for a long time and obediently didn't read any further. As I just couldn't figure out exactly what I was seeking, I abandoned the study. Some 30 years later, I was reminded of the course and, because by then I did know the answer to the question, I re-enrolled and studied the valuable information for many years.

What Do You Most Desire?

This remains the one question, important above all else, that you, too, must answer: *What do I most desire?*

The emotive word *desire* includes all you could possibly require to live with joy, comfort and ease—part of my daily mantra—with no hint of want or neediness. Most importantly, whatever you're aiming for becomes wonderfully energized when you truly desire it. Don't forget you deserve *any* thing—spiritual, emotional, physical or material—that to you is part of an exceptional life.

Desire is essential for manifestation and is one of the effective power words to use when formulating your goals. It evokes passion, enthusiasm, excitement. After all, you wouldn't say, *I desire a cup of tea!* It's far too strong a word to use for something you'd simply like.

Dare to dream—dream big and in Technicolor. Imagine and clearly define your dream of all that you'd like out of life. Not what you're willing to accept but rather what will make your life extraordinary. Create your own vision of how you'd like to be living next year, in five years' time, in ten or more. Then ignite it with a burning desire to create every facet that together constitutes your perfect outcome, no matter what it takes. Advance confidently in the direction of your dreams. Don't let anything or anyone shake your knowing that you don't have to accept a life less ordinary as most people do. Then you're able to contribute so much more to others and the world.

Have fire in your desire and never let it dim or worse still, go out. As Napoleon Hill said, the starting point of all achievement is desire. Using the analogy of a physical fire, the more logs you put on it, the greater the resulting heat. The energy of your inner burning desire is the most powerful creative force you can have.

The answer to the question *What do I most desire?* has to be precise—vague goals get vague results. Imagine going into a travel agent, offering your credit card and saying, *Please give me a ticket.*

Where to? you are asked.

I don't know—just give me a ticket! you reply. Guess what? You won't be going anywhere any time soon.

No doubt you're finding it very challenging to formulate an answer that encompasses everything and yet is precise. After many years of working with this conundrum myself, I came up with a technique that ticks all the boxes.

Focus Your Desires: The Diamond of Life

Take a moment now to write down as many specifics as quickly come to mind, such as more loving friendships, relationships, a soul mate/partner, better health, job satisfaction, excitement, happiness, success, peace of mind, fulfillment, greater quality of life, to be more spiritual—and yes, to have more money, a nicer house, a new car, and so on. Don't hold back.

Now put your list to one side for a moment, and answer the following question: What is the most precious and valuable gem of all? As the old song goes, a diamond is a girl's—and boy's—best friend! I use the analogy of a diamond for two reasons: firstly, its origin as a rough piece of "rock" gives little hint of its hidden potential to become an exquisite thing of beauty. Yet someone with the necessary know-how, skills and tools, can transform the dull rock into a precious gem of sparkling, multi-faceted brilliance. Similarly, giving you the means to transform your life to reveal your true magnificence is the object of this guidebook. In line with this, it's interesting that sometimes we refer to a person as a "diamond-in-the-rough," suggesting they have hidden, latent potential.

Secondly, all the diamond's brilliant facets that make up its full light-reflecting perfection, provide an appropriate analogy for how I laser-focus my goals and condense a huge raft of details. I've found that this concept easily and most effectively itemizes the numerous specific items of my desire list while also being ideal for expressing complex overall outcomes.

Now look at your list again. You'll discover that every item you've listed can be categorized under four main headings: *love*, *abundance*, *wellbeing* and *successful fulfillment*. The anagram of the words *love*, *abundance*, *wellbeing* and *success* makes LAWS, an easy way to remember a lot of detail. It provides a perfect check-list for conveniently formulating your goals, now and in the future.

The diamond analogy has a complementary aspect to your list. Think of the geometric form of a diamond with its four equal sides. If you write one of the four words along each side, you've got four quadrants in which you can note all the specific facets from your list.

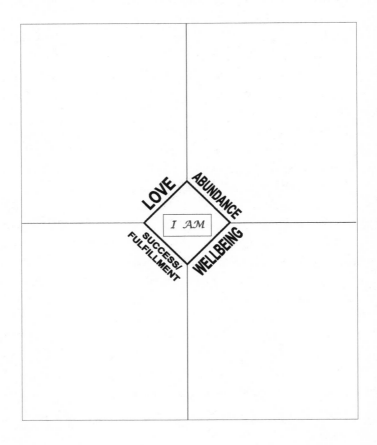

Using this *Perfect Diamond of Life* tool (available for reproduction in Appendix) gives you a stunningly simple way of having a plan of action to live by, the only sure way to move steadily towards achieving the life of your dreams. It offers a design framework that makes it easy for you to get clear on exactly what your perfect outcomes are that ultimately lead to enjoying the highest "diamond-standard" of living possible.

Whenever I decree my overall outcome, I simply say the phrase, *My Perfect Diamond of Life.* Every tiny detail is then covered, and I don't have to try and remember all the specifics. I also use this beautifully concise yet all-encompassing phrase when I give thanks morning and night for my Heaven on Earth existence.

The Perfect Diamond of Life

In the next four chapters, I will go into each of the four categories described for the Diamond of Life, so you can see what is included as well as how to identify any "off" switches lurking in your subconscious mind. This designed framework lays the ground-work for your ongoing successful manifestation of everything that makes up a life you'd love to live.

You'll see how I've titled each of the four chapters with what is probably the most powerful decree you can use, as well as the shortest sentence in the English language—I AM. Using I AM immediately puts the decree under your highest power source, and allows your HS to be in charge—and intervene for your most beneficial outcome if necessary. It also helps remind you that your limited third dimensional self can relax and let go—*Let go and let God*—referring to your God-Self. And most importantly, you are creating the state of mind for the Miracle Effect that allows miracles to occur—and that empowers you to become a *Miracle Magnet!* Let's look at what is necessary for each of the four categories to reach its greatest brilliance and manifestation potential.

CHAPTER 16
I AM Limitless Love

A lifetime without Love is of no account.
Love is the Water of Life
Drink it down with heart and soul. Rumi

Love governs the first quadrant of the *Perfect Diamond of Life*. Before you fill this quadrant in with specific items from your list, I suggest you do the following preparation:

Preparation

Review the following thoughts and check those that have an instant emotional charge of recognition for you:

- *No-one could love me if they knew what I'm really like .....*
- *I'm always overlooked or left out .....*
- *No-one really cares .....*
- *I'm lonely – unlovable .....*
- *I don't deserve love/ I'm not worthy enough .....*
- *People always leave me .....*

Do any of these sound familiar? If so, remember what to do before taking another step: Apply *Emergency Mind CPR* (see Chapter 13). Do the same if the phrases have triggered other unwanted memories. If you sense that the mistaken belief is so deeply rooted or goes back beyond this life experience, then apply the technique for eradicating seed causes (see Chapter 9) to make sure. You don't want to continue carrying this baggage any longer. If you don't deal with self-sabotaging beliefs as you go, then they will thwart all your attempts to live in the exquisite state of Limitless Love you are entitled to enjoy.

Love Is .....

Love is such an overused word in English. The Greeks have two words, *agape* and *eros*. Agape is divine, unifying spiritual love that never changes and includes brotherly/sisterly love as well as love for other life-forms. Eros refers to sensual, sexual love and relationships that can change, and is often impermanent. Enjoying both kinds of love is a wonderful gift of being human and the highest emotional frequency we as humans can experience.

As is now well known, love is as essential as food. This was demonstrated when sadly during the last century's aftermath of wars, many babies were orphaned. Too late it was found that even if they were fed and clothed, many starved to death because they didn't receive human love, touching and nurturing.

What expands the more you give it out? We're so conditioned to think that whatever we give must deplete our supply, but this is not so with love. Quite the opposite in fact, as giving love expands your experience and store of love. The more love you give, the more your capacity to be loved, lovable and loving increases. How you do this is limitless, and the more loving you are, the more you attract only loving people and situations into your life.

Forgiveness

Although mentioned earlier, forgiveness is so important that it's worth re-visiting. Love and un-forgiveness cannot coexist. You are either in the all-encompassing state of love or you are not. Holding un-forgiveness of any kind, either towards others or yourself, cancels out love. It's like thinking it's possible to be partly pregnant. Furthermore, un-forgiveness completely stops the flow of Love-Light Power from your HS. So use the Universal Laws as presented earlier in Chapter 6 to make sure you have forgiven everyone now and in the past, still living or not—and yourself—for every incident, situation or relationship that has ever challenged you.

Enjoying More Love in Your Life

No matter whether you desire to have a loving partner or soulmate, to have more loving friends, to be greatly loved and appreciated, to love your work and your life much more, there is just one cardinal rule: to receive and experience greater love in your life, you have to *give* love, *be* more loving and lovable. Selflessness, loving thoughts and kind words increase your love vibration; selfish, critical, judgmental or envious thoughts dramatically decrease the most precious and powerfully healing vibrational frequency on earth.

If you give unconditional love and support, you will receive love and support, though not necessarily from those you give it to. If you give blessings, you will receive blessings; if you give loyalty, you will receive loyalty. The universal *Law of Energy Exchange* works infallibly at the vibrational level you're aligned with, often collecting more expressions of the same level on its way back to you—yes, even miracles.

Gratitude

Gratitude is a powerful expression of love. You can't help but feel loving when your attitude is one of gratitude. What's more, it obeys the *Law of Expansion*. Lovingly focusing on what you already have sends the message to the universe that you appreciate your gifts of life. This grateful attitude energy not only maintains but ensures you get more of the best. It opens the floodgates, so more of what you love and enjoy can pour into physical, emotional, mental and spiritual forms. Quite often, when I'm thinking about all the beautiful things in my life I'm grateful for, I become so overwhelmed with love that it brings tears of joy to my eyes.

Maintaining a state of love-filled gratefulness leads to inner calm and peace of mind that brings the added bonus of acting as de-stressors. More love equals less stress. Along with contentment, the grateful attitude habit is an intrinsic aspect of developing your Miracle-Effect, an important foundation for creating the environment for miracles to occur.

Part of my morning and nightly gratitude ritual is saying or thinking: *I'm so happy and grateful for the love that fills my life; for all those who bless and enrich my life past, present and future; for my wonderful body that serves me so well in optimum health and function; for satisfying success and fulfillment in all I do; for abundance of all things that help make my life heaven on earth, and for all the loving support and ongoing miracles I enjoy.*

The added benefit of this appreciation ritual is that I give myself two daily doses of endorphins!

Count Your Blessings

Count your blessings one by one is another powerful way of expressing your love of the gift of life. Look around and give thanks for all the blessings you enjoy, each and every day. Get into the habit of being mindful of the many small things in life that you take for granted. This creates peace and harmony in your mind, and keeps you centered on what's already good and wonderful, a sure-fire way to keep open to receiving more of the same. *Where your focus goes, the energy flows.*

However, remember that feeling thankful doesn't imply being complacent. Keep aiming to expand yourself, so you unleash more and more of your latent potential. The more you do so, the more you have to give to the world. To grow and evolve is everyone's true life purpose, so each of us can make a difference no matter how small. As a being of divine origin, you are destined for greatness no matter how long or how many lives it takes. How many more lives do you want to take hiding your true, unlimited, love-light, Miracle Me self?

Contentment and Joy

Another facet of love is contentment. What's the content of your life? If it's filled with appreciation for all the good you have to enjoy right in this moment, inner joy inevitably bubbles up and radiates throughout your whole being. So often we forget to focus only on what is right and beautiful in our life. Instead, we let ourselves become mesmerized with the small percentage of what may not be pleasing. Not a good plan.

Key aspects of fully living love include being content with what you have, no matter the circumstances. For me, one example is that after living in family-sized houses as most of my peers still do, I now live happily in a tiny cottage unit that I lovingly call my "home haven." I totally agree with Confucius, who put it perfectly thus: *I live in a small house but I look out on a huge world.*

Loving What You Do

Loving everything you do keeps your vibrational frequencies in the highest range possible. Yes, even the housework, because it reminds you to be grateful that you have the luxury of a house to clean when millions are denied this basic necessity.

Love every aspect of your life, even the challenges as they arise. If you look past appearances and seek the gift, or at least the learning, in each one, then you'll find you can quickly regain your equilibrium and inner peace.

More Love Expressions

- Helping, supporting and/or serving others both individually or through community and global groups that work with those less fortunate.
- Caring for and loving animals, plants, gardens, our shared environment, beautiful country and world.
- A neat share-my-love habit I've developed is to send "love darts" to bless anyone I see when I'm out shopping or driving, or anyone I think of, even to people I see on TV.

> • Help make the world a better place by spontaneous random acts of kindness every day. Kindness begets kindness. When someone does a kind thing for you, you feel inspired to pass that kindness along, to pay it forward. Watch what happens when you do a kindness to someone. The Dalai Lama says, *Be kind whenever possible. It is always possible.*

Love Decrees

To expand your Limitless Love experiences, you can itemize several smaller specific aims in your list at the outset, as well as an overall perfect outcome. For example, if the top of your list is to attract a soul mate, then by all means decree this. And don't forget to always include the word *perfect*. Then you don't have to keep listing all the qualities you desire or be concerned you might leave out a very important one.

A dear friend of mine who was unaware of this magical power word, decreed some years ago to meet her soul mate, now her husband. She got everything on her detailed list but unfortunately hadn't thought of including good health. Sadly her husband has had to have endless major surgeries including a major transplant, and suffers overall poor health that requires constant nursing, severely limiting their quality of life on a day-to-day basis.

Many years ago, I decided I'd like more than one special girl-friend because I'd grown up a lonely, shy and introverted child whose manner created entirely the wrong impression and pushed others away. More than once, I was nicknamed the Ice Queen. I found it extremely difficult to make friends. With all the evacuation moves during WWII and subsequently emigrating from England to New Zealand, I ended up attending fifteen schools altogether, which certainly didn't help. In all those schools I only managed to have three best friends. This loneliness carried on well into my adult life.

As I began acquiring the precious knowledge and tools I now share, I realized I could do something to change this unhappy state. My first challenge was consciously allowing myself to feel vulnerable and overcome my fear of rejection by reaching out in friendly and approachable ways. Slowly, I became able to radiate my genuine inner loving nature that was always there, but which I'd learned to hide as a defense against so often feeling on the outside. Eventually, from my early thirties on, I began to create the outcome I so dearly desired. In more recent years I supported my intention by decreeing that I would attract an ever-growing circle of many special loving and supportive friends. That is exactly what I enjoy today.

While it's always more powerful to create outcomes and decrees in your own words, many of my students ask for my personal versions to inspire them. To ensure they remain fresh and alive, I don't stick to the exact same wording every time, but here's an example of my original outcome decree:

With my full Higher Self Power, I decree that I always enjoy an ever-increasing abundance of love to give and receive from my dear family and loving, loyal friends, acquaintances, colleagues, students, neighbors—all who bless and enrich my life, past, present and future. I give grateful thanks that it is so.

As I now enjoy this manifested outcome, I regularly include it in my gratitude prayers by re-wording it thus: *I AM so happy and grateful for the ongoing expanding love that fills my life, love I enjoy giving and receiving from all who bless and enrich my life, past, present and future.*

Sometimes I add the specifics of family, growing circle of friends, colleagues, acquaintances and so on. This practice keeps the energy vibrantly alive and active.

CHAPTER 17
I AM Amazing Abundance

Abundance is the word in the second quadrant of your *Perfect Diamond of Life*. Before filling in this quadrant with specific items from your list, I suggest you do the following preparation:

Preparation

As before, check these common misperceptions to see which ones ring a bell for you:

- *Rich people aren't happy or nice .....*
- *Money doesn't grow on trees .....*
- *There's not enough to go round .....*
- *Money is hard to come by.......*
- *I mustn't be greedy .....*
- *Everything is too expensive ...... I can't afford this .....*
- *You can't be spiritual if you're wealthy.*

Remember what to do? Don't allow yourself to own these beliefs that come from other people any longer—apply *Emergency Mind CPR* and de-activate the seed causes if you feel that is necessary. Poverty-consciousness seed causes are deep-seated for many people, having often been repeatedly strengthened in several lifetimes. So many of us have spent lives as nuns and monks for example, which required us to take vows of poverty. Even if you cannot remember this, many people find it's beneficial to use the techniques for de-activating seed causes outlined in Chapter 9 to cover this possibility.

The Power of "I Can't"

Whenever you think or say *I can't*, your subconscious mind believes you and closes all doors to creating or attracting what you require or desire. Instead, flip the switch and say, *How can I?* This question opens the door, so new ideas can come through from your subconscious mind as it sets to work to find an answer. It also allows your HS to help you reconfigure your mind so you can achieve your desire.

Try this: Imagine abundance, including money, as a limitless, self-perpetuating ocean. You are invited to take however much you would like. What kind of apparatus would you use to take your share?

Did you immediately think of using a cup, a bucket, or even a wheelbarrow? How about plugging directly into the ocean and turning on the tap for your supply? Think garden hose, for example. If you chose anything less, you now have another major insight into your subconscious programs of lack, limitation and scarcity.

Limitless Supply

Work on accepting that the universe is limitless, that the Quantum Field contains all potential, together with all information regarding any kind of possible perfect creation that is waiting for you to bring into form. Only *you* can close the floodgates on this unending flow that's easily accessible when you allow your HS to partner with you. Only *you* can dam up the limitless supply of all abundance and good, and prevent it from continuously flowing into whatever form of manifestation you choose.

I personally give thanks each day for all the wonderful forms of abundance I enjoy that create my Heaven on Earth kind of life. Here is an example of how I word my gratitude:

> *I give thanks for the abundance of love to give and receive; abundance of peace and tranquility in my little home haven; abundance of beauty all around me and in the world I look out on; abundance of health, wellbeing, mental acuity and energy; abundance of fulfillment and success I continue to enjoy in everything I do both personally and as my Soul Service; abundance of lovely things to do and experience, like social events with friends or attending a ballet; abundance of money continuously flowing into my accounts, so I live with comfort and ease …*

Why not take a moment now and do the same for the abundance you already enjoy? Write out your own words of gratitude, listing all the ways you are thankful for your life. Imprinting this all-important limitless, expanding and ongoing abundance into your conscious and subconscious minds is a Miracle Effect essential to I AM Mastery—and to create the life you deeply long to have.

Manifesting Abundance

Many decades ago when I was new to the concept of manifesting, I tested many theories I came across. As a solo mum bringing up an adolescent son with no support apart from the meager government benefit, manifesting abundance was at the top of my list. I followed all the methods of affirmation, visualization, and the like that I'd read about. Yes, I manifested abundance, but because I hadn't specified what kind, I soon became swamped with an abundance of work—more than I could handle. This unexpected outcome quickly taught me the importance of being specific when attempting to manifest a desire.

After many years teaching only ballet, I had travelled around countries in Europe and discovered their folkloric dance traditions. These enthralled me so much that I enthusiastically studied and specialized in ethnic dance. This led to me forming an international theatre dance company, *Korobushka*, that was unique in New Zealand and so for 21 years I specialized in producing stage performances. Interestingly, this passion led to another meaningful lesson in manifestation. In 1982, I was awarded a major New Zealand Government Arts Council Study Travel grant that enabled me to go to several countries of my choice to learn more about their folkloric dance and stage choreographies, costuming, music and production techniques. The aim was to bring back first-hand knowledge to use in my performing company and expand its repertoire.

My company not only did stage performances but also many community and school programs as well. These latter activities were behind the reason I was honored in the 1990 New Year's Royal Honors List, with a Queen's Service Medal (QSM) for services to the community.

Again, I diligently applied the manifestation techniques I'd learned, and, exactly as the commitment quote promised, all kinds of miraculous support appeared. However, what I didn't know at that time was to include the word *perfect*. The trip turned out to be one of the most difficult and challenging experiences of my whole life—even scary at times, especially in places like Russia and Hungary that were still under tight communist rule. Yes, I learned much about dancing, but even more important, I learned the hard way how to allow my God-Self to work through me and provide miraculous solutions to seemingly hopeless situations. The first step of "letting go and letting God," I discovered, was to relax and smile while handing it over to a higher source for help.

One of the worst scenarios happened in Budapest when one evening I found myself locked out of the apartment I'd rented. In 1982, English was almost unknown in Hungary, so I had no way of getting around and finding a place to stay—on my own that is. Being unable to communicate with anyone made me feel like an alien on another planet. There I stood, frightened and alone in a huge city with no idea of where I would spend the night.

Thankfully, a lady appeared in answer to my desperate inner pleas for higher help—a true God-send. Because Hungarian is a unique language with no common roots or similarities to any other, she and I could only communicate using gestures. International visitors were extremely rare back then in poverty-stricken Hungary, but this wonderful lady trusted me enough to allow me to sleep the night on her horsehair sofa. If only I'd worked on manifesting the trip using the word *perfect*.

Money and Spirituality

The big issue for so many people, especially for those intent on their spiritual progress, is money. Many centuries of conditioning by religious teaching is the main source of the mindset that it's noble to be poor. *If you want to be spiritual, then it's essential to live in poverty*, is how this powerful form of control goes.

But what is noble about being so consumed with the desperate need for enough money to survive that there's no time left for anything else, let alone appreciating the gift of life and following spiritual pursuits? The best way I've heard for expressing this mistaken belief is: *If you're wealthy and enjoying a loving sexual relationship, then you can't possibly be spiritual. To be spiritual, you have to be horny and broke!*

The Secret of Money Is Having Some

Money is only one facet of abundance, but because it is such an issue for many let's have a deeper look at it. First, it helps to remember that money is simply a tangible form of energy exchange. If a Martian arrived on earth and was given hundred dollar bills, he could quite easily use them to get a fire started. To him, they'd just be bits of paper.

Money is simply a form of exchange for the energy we put out, which is why I have a problem with the oft-stated belief about achieving a desired result (especially among those newer on the spiritual path), of: *Oh, I don't have to do anything. The universe will provide.*

The immutable *Law of Energy Exchange* clearly explains why this belief is flawed. We receive back energy (in some form) in direct proportion to what we expend, depending upon our intention and attitude behind it.

Special Universal Money Laws

There are a two more Universal Laws that particularly apply to manifesting money, useful to know so you don't inadvertently get in your own way by not applying them: *The Law of Circulation* and the *Law of Tithing*

The Law of Circulation is partner to the *Law of Energy Exchange* and states that the energy you send out in any form always comes back to you, like the outward and return movement of drawing a circle. Further, what comes back is multiplied because it magnetically attracts like energy, so keep mindful of your thoughts and feelings when giving out money. Don't allow yourself to be fearful of making payments, especially bills. Pay confidently, making sure you do so with an attitude of appreciation and blessing rather than with resentment. Negative energy blocks the possibility of money continuously streaming in, while positive energy creates the space and movement for more to continue flowing into your hands or accounts effortlessly and abundantly.

Energy needs to keep moving and circulating, not be stored up just for the sake of having a big bank balance. Have you noticed an increasing number of wealthy people today are living with this more enlightened awareness? Instead of accumulating more and more wealth, they consistently give out what they don't need to support humanitarian projects and those less fortunate than themselves. As a result, they are noticeably happier for keeping money circulating in this way, as well as helping make the world a better place for more people.

I learned about the Law of Tithing when, many years ago when I was a struggling solo parent wondering how I was going to pay the bills, I asked Holy Spirit what I should do. The answer was certainly not what I expected. It was suggested I take on a second child to support as part of an overseas programme that helps third world countries. I had managed to keep supporting one—but two? Before I had time for this to sink in, an additional suggestion came: Have 500 bookmarks printed with the I AM Decree on them to give out free of charge.

To say I was gobsmacked is an understatement. For a while, I wasn't brave enough to do either, but seeing I was learning to trust Spirit at that time, I finally plucked up enough courage and did both. Very soon afterwards, work came in, money owing to me was paid, and all was well—that is, until the next time.

I must have been a slow learner because the following year I was in the same predicament and asked again for guidance. I received a similar answer, except this time instead of bookmarks, HS suggested I start regular, conscious tithing, even with the minimal and erratic income I had. It worked, of course, and so I was introduced to the magic of tithing.

The principle underlying tithing is that giving fearlessly and joyfully releases a flow of energy that opens the way for more to come in. Fear of not having enough, that the source will dry up or is limited, restricts—even stops—the flow, as I'd already learned the hard way.

Tithing affirms your confidence and certainty—not just hope or belief—of knowing there's always plenty more whenever you require it. It's also a tangible way of giving thanks and appreciation for your life and all you have and enjoy. Keep in mind that the *Law of Gratitude* expands what you focus on.

Tithing is giving approximately ten percent of your income (or what you receive from any source), with genuine love, joy and pleasure. (The words *tithe* and *ten* both have the same root.) You give with no expectation of a return, not even thanks. This is the reason why secret or anonymous tithing is preferable. Tithing can also be done partly in the form of giving time and/or expertise; you can apply the "5+5 rule" of giving five percent in money and five percent in your time.

To support the giving principle, aim to give a gift every day. It may be as little as a smile, a compliment, a kind word, a random act of kindness, paying for someone's parking or cup of coffee. Ask yourself daily: *How or what can I give today?*

I've Saved the Best Tips for Last

- *The "no limits" mantra*. A dear friend of mine once made a throw-away remark that stuck in my mind. He said that he never let money limit him, and his life demonstrated this truth, even though he wasn't born wealthy and had not inherited any money. So I now live by the same mantra as the icing on my financial abundance cake. I've re-worded it to get rid of the negative word and give it more punch.

  Here it is—I say it often with conviction and a big grin: *I refuse to allow money to limit me!*

- *Focus only on the outcome, not a specific income.* In other words, be aware of what you really require and desire money for. Isn't it so you can live perfectly in comfort and ease? This has to include being able to effortlessly pay all your bills and expenses, buy the necessities of life, enjoy treats and special occasions, do what you love to do. Notice how the magic word *perfectly* ensures all this. The secret is, don't limit yourself to an amount. Allow HS to supply all you require and desire, and you'll often receive much, much more.

- *Allow for extra abundance.* If instead, you focus on a particular amount, you won't allow marvelous, extra abundance, even financial miracles, into your life. Even for a specific item that has a certain price tag, like a car for example, why not be free and limitless by simply stating your desired outcome for the perfect car? You can include details such as perfect mileage and age, the make and any other details important to you if you wish. But if you allow HS to work through you, then the outcome is likely to be far more wonderful than you could have imagined was possible—and you may not even have to buy it yourself.

• **Get out of your own way and let HS work miracles.** Holding only the perfect outcome as your aim will help you get out of your own way, so HS can answer in ways that transcend the usual monetary requirement. I remember Ava, a lady who came to my meditation group two decades ago, telling me she was putting out her need for a reliable car to buy to take her to work. Some weeks later when I saw her again, I asked her had she manifested the car yet.

"Oh yes," she replied, "I've got another car."

"That's great manifesting," I replied enthusiastically.

Without missing a beat Ava answered, "Oh no, it doesn't count."

Puzzled, I asked her why. "Because my brother gave it to me!"

The moral of the story is this: refuse to allow yourself to create limits by becoming attached to your outcomes appearing only through the means you can envision. Never forget that HS can work miracles through whatever instrument or person that is best for you. All you have to do is remember to be grateful.

Manifesting Money by Different Methods

Having read this chapter, it may not sit right with you to manifest money based solely on trust as I have described. If, for example, you feel more comfortable with the usual methods, then please know that it's no reflection on you if you choose to continue doing them instead.

When I was a school-teacher, we knew each child had to reach what was termed their "reading readiness" level before they could master reading. So it is with this somewhat unorthodox, money-manifesting methodology. If or when you're ready to adopt it, you will know. Meanwhile it's better not to timidly or half-heartedly give it a try, as fear and doubt could leave you worse off. Far better to continue using what works best for you. Having said that, using some of the information in this guide to begin changing your mindset would be advantageous—and this applies to the self-healing suggestions, too.

To illustrate the readiness point, about nine years ago, before I adopted the Miracle Effect approach, a close family member who was concerned about my financial difficulties (as I myself was) suggested I get some budgeting advice. He himself works with a strict budget, having several bank accounts for regularly saving money so he is always ready to cover various living expenses as they arise as well as providing for the future. This method is perfect for him and gives him peace of mind.

Off I went to the senior citizens' budgeting help department, and after answering a huge raft of questions and listing every tiny expense, including possible unexpected extras that may or may not occur in the future, the lady worked out a financial budget given my small pension and erratic income. No prizes for guessing the conclusion. With a substantial mortgage and living alone, my projected outgoings exceeded my income—a result I'd already sensed was likely.

Mulling over this on the way home, I found myself feeling not worried but amused. This was my turning point. I had reached the necessary stage of readiness, ready to "walk my talk" by putting into practice the spiritual knowledge and principles I accepted as true.

When I got home, I went into the garden with the two copies of the budget figures that now represented to me the limited, third-dimensional beliefs I was now ready to delete. I made a little ceremony, and I burnt them! I watched the last vestiges of my early conditioning and fear-filled mindset around money represented by the smoke, return to the nothingness from whence they came. In that defining moment, I consciously decided to use what I've been teaching and writing about, trusting completely in my Higher Self power and the Miracle Effect.

Granted, I live a modest lifestyle, but from that time on, I have never again struggled to make ends meet nor wanted for anything. As I confidently began to rely solely on my HS to answer my perfect abundance and outcome (not income) decrees, together with regular monetary and time tithing, money miracles started occurring unasked through all sorts of avenues and people, far beyond the expected energy exchange. These blessings continue to this day. The more freely and fearlessly I live, the more I receive. I have proved and confirmed for myself that living limitlessly as a Miracle Me expression of my true Self covers every aspect of life, including money. Yes, even including money.

CHAPTER 18

I AM Wonderful Wellbeing

Well-being is the word in the third quadrant of your *Perfect Diamond of Life*. Before filling in this quadrant with specific items from your list, I suggest you do the following preparation:

Preparation

As before, I've provided a short check-list to get you thinking about your subconscious programming around health and wellbeing:

- *I have my mother/father/family's genes, so I'm bound to get .....*
- *Each year I always get .....*
- *Doctor/pills/surgery are the only things that can make me well .....*
- *Someone else or some healing modality will fix it ... ...*
- <u>*My*</u> *condition* – <u>*my*</u> *illness* – <u>*my*</u> *certain prognosis .....*

You know what to do if any of these detrimental beliefs resonate, and if they trigger other ones to come into your mind. Now let's clarify some of the above that you may be wondering about.

Sabotaging Beliefs Around Wellbeing

The first belief, that the genes you inherit determine your future, is now scientifically proven to be false. Leading pioneer in genetics Dr. Bruce Lipton has proven beyond a doubt that we are not controlled by our genes. His decades of research show that instead of being a victim of your genes, you can be a master of your own body and fate, able to create a life overflowing with all you desire—resulting in what both Dr. Lipton and I call *Heaven on Earth*.

Dr. Lipton's breakthrough work is known as the new science of *epigenetics,* which literally means "control above the genes." Only around 5 percent or less of our genes are fixed. The other 95 percent are changeable, dependent upon what environmental factors influence their activity. This means that our gene activity is constantly being modified in response to our life experiences and perceptions. So even if you have an inherited disposition or tendency towards certain diseases, this does not mean you have to manifest any of them, whether or not other family members have done so. If you're interested in understanding this liberating new science better and how to use it, I strongly recommend Bruce's wonderful book, *The Biology of Belief.* It may well help change your life.

The second sabotaging belief in the list above is especially prevalent during winter time. This is when so often you hear people saying they always get so many colds during the year, or, when asked if they've had the flu, they answer, *Not yet.* Tacit expectations like these reflect your unconscious beliefs. Changing your mind and beliefs moves you from victim mode to victor, as does ascending your vibrations. A high-frequency, harmonious person is never vibrating at the same rate and level as a germ or virus.

The third and fourth beliefs aren't meant to imply that some valid conditions don't require and respond to medical intervention or prescriptions. However, in some cases, there may be other possibilities. But for them to work, you have to be open to that possibility first. I still chuckle at how I allowed myself to be locked in—*almost*—to the belief that major knee surgery was necessary, simply because I'd subconsciously accepted that the best solution was to hand my power over to someone else.

The last belief on the list highlights the fact that there's a tendency for many people to proudly own their illness like a badge of honor. You may recall the *Law of Acceptance* saying that if you accept something, it's yours. Owning an illness means that there's no room for any possible self-healing to occur. Your choice.

Wellbeing and Wonder

I deliberately use the term *wellbeing* rather than health because you can still enjoy a deep sense of wellbeing, even if your health is not perfect or you have some disability. Many people are demonstrating this by only focusing on the positive functioning aspects of their bodies and refusing to allow what is not so good to dominate their thoughts and lives. This is real wisdom in action and results in having wellbeing.

The other word, *wonder*, which to me is part of the wellbeing equation, refers to becoming aware and conscious of the marvelous creation that is your body—and daily thanking it for providing the vehicle that is perfectly suited to take you through this physical life journey. How all of your body's highly complex functions work ceaselessly 24/7 without a thought on your part is a wonder of this world. So look with wonder at that which serves you so well.

I've found it has been helpful to ask myself the question: *What is essential for my wellbeing?* My answer not only includes optimum health, pain-free functioning and mobility of my body, but also things like my living environment. Silence, peace, and tranquility are vital for my everyday wellbeing, as is being able to live with an enjoyable level of comfort and ease. Having defined these, I'm now able to include them as part of my perfect outcomes.

My Self-Healings

I described earlier how a few years ago I manifested not one but two degenerative bone conditions that are accepted as being inevitably crippling because they are medically untreatable. Applying the information you have learned about in this book, I healed them both.

The first condition was a very painful lower back degeneration which used to run in the female line of my mother's family. She manifested it as did my aunt. Eventually I did too, and like them, I was told that according to the MRI scan there was nothing that could be done except be put on ever-increasing pain medication.

When the condition kicked in, I found I was unable to do simple, everyday things. I couldn't stand long enough to clean my teeth because after a few seconds, the pain was too intense. Even leaning on the bench, I wasn't able to stay on my feet to wash the dishes, let alone make a cup of tea. Every small movement aggravated the pain.

When I read the report of my MRI results, I made a decision that flipped a switch in my mind. I decided to choose *not to accept* this awful diagnosis. The thought of this being my life from then onwards just wasn't an option. From that defining moment, using all the knowledge I had gained thus far, I set about creating practices based upon my inner knowing that as a Divine Being, it is absolutely possible to rise above the physical level and, with the invincible help of my I AM Higher Self, allow the pain from the condition to heal.

It worked. The necessary understanding and techniques I used to heal my lower back degeneration pain are all in this book. It didn't happen overnight. But with unwavering perseverance and refusing to allow any doubt cross my mind that my desired outcome of being pain-free and mobile was certain, I AM now exactly that. As a footnote, the normal, expected progression of this condition results in ultimately being completely unable to stand upright or walk. Sadly, my aunt went down that painful, debilitating route, ending up in a wheelchair and finally bed-ridden.

How did I do it? First, I accepted that it was possible to Self-heal despite the medical diagnosis. I set to work to demonstrate I AM my own healer by using the power of my HS and the many Miracle-Effect techniques I've already outlined including de-activating the seed cause. Picturing my I AM Light Body laid vertically over my physical body as you've learned to do in the Axiatonal Lines process, while chanting the Divine Name *Yod-Heh-Vod-Heh* to re-activate my DNA God-Code (see Appendix) was my daily practice. I created I AM decrees that reinforced the truth that my back was already restored to perfect pain-free function. I strengthened their power with daily chanting the Divine Name (as described in Chapter 11), while specifically holding the picture of my perfect outcome having already been created as I did so. As *A Course in Miracles* principle states, miracles rearrange perception. I adapted one of its simple yet powerful sayings to change my original faulty perception, chanting it as often as possible: *I AM not my body, I AM free, I AM as God created me.*

Other mind-changing *ACIM* principles explain that miracles heal because they transcend the body by denying body-identification and affirming the perfection of spirit-identification. By raising yourself to the sphere of celestial order beyond physical laws, you are perfect. My own not just one but two separate healing experiences brilliantly illustrated this truth.

The second medically untreatable condition occurred about four years later when my left foot completely collapsed, so the bones grated against each other and on the ground. This meant that yet again I couldn't even stand, let alone walk without excruciating pain, though this time coming from my foot. Just putting the slightest weight on it was agony. I vividly remember watching everyone else nonchalantly standing and walking effortlessly without a care in the world, something we all tend to take for granted. I admit feeling envious of them all at the beginning. However, once I got over the brief "poor me" interlude, I got back on track working to self-heal the condition, seeing there was no other option if I wished to enjoy a normal life. I applied the same understanding and techniques as I've described previously. Today I continue to walk effortlessly and pain-free and can even gently dance—gifts beyond price.

This condition was a congenital one I'd brought with me into this life. I was born with exceedingly weak, flat feet resulting in an ungainly walk that developed into constant pain in the soles by the age of eight. An orthopedic specialist looked at my feet almost as a curiosity because their condition was so unusual and then told my mother he thought the best thing for me would be ballet. I was over the moon because since the age of about three, all I had wanted to do was dance. But life in post-war England was hard, and my folks couldn't afford lessons. Ballet had to wait until after we had emigrated to New Zealand—but that's another story. The specialist arranged for electric-shock treatment at the hospital which was all he could offer. The treatment felt like torture, and I dreaded each visit, though it eventually helped to make the condition slightly more bearable.

Finally, learning ballet at age 13 was my life's dream come true. I didn't care that I looked like a huge heavy-weight in the beginners' class of dainty little girls 6 or 7 years younger than myself. Through a series of minor miracles of support by the right teachers who recognized my teaching potential, I was fast-tracked through the necessary training to become qualified. Sadly, I accepted that this body was never designed to be a ballerina. When I'd just turned 16, I opened my first ballet studio, delighting in being able to teach and pass on my love of dance.

Teaching dancing for over 40 years was my passion with the bonus of strengthening my feet, thus keeping deterioration and pain at bay. After teaching ballet for 10 years I continued my love of dancing by specializing in ethnic or folkloric dance as I've already described, both performing and later teaching and running my own theatre company until 1990. You can imagine my distress when the original weakness returned due to lack of hard exercise, resulting in a total bone collapse of my weaker foot. This incredibly painful and debilitating new condition arose because some years previously, I'd stopped dancing to concentrate on what I've really come to do in this life—my spiritual work and service.

The reason I've shared the history of this condition is to highlight the fact that even long-term or lifelong physical imperfections can still be Self-healed from higher dimensional frequencies and viewpoints. In my case, fulfilling my innate desire to dance worked beautifully on the third-dimensional level for many years. But a totally different mindset and approach was required for a permanent result to occur later on.

I did ask HS, rather petulantly I admit, why I'd brought these two serious congenital, potentially limiting conditions into this life with me. In hindsight, the answer was obvious. *If you didn't have anything to work on, then you wouldn't bother!* How true for my Self-mastery progress, but it has also meant I've been able to help others so much more. And yes, the x-rays and MRI scans still show nothing has changed physically, proving to me that by working from one's fifth-dimensional I AM Higher Self, anything can be transcended—*hallelu-YAH*!

Rejuvenation and Agelessness

A few weeks ago, the hospital nurse looked down at my file in front of her, then looked up at me with a puzzled expression. She checked again and then asked me for my date of birth. When I told her, she was genuinely surprised to see that it did in fact correspond with the age given. "You certainly don't look anything like 76," she exclaimed. "You look much younger and vastly different from most of the people I see of that age."

I'm sharing this little incident to illustrate the point that even without holding a rejuvenation focus, permanent youthfulness in mind and body are some of the amazing side-effects of working from a Miracle-Effect perspective.

Ageing is a mistake of the intellect. You will grow older, but you don't have to "age." Thinking of yourself as youthful and ageless imprints this as an accomplished fact in the Quantum Field. Don't forget to include perfect brain function, mental acuity, memory, understanding and awareness as part of your wellbeing and healthy life goal.

I always include the following words in my wellbeing and gratitude decrees: ... *continual rejuvenation, youthfulness and agelessness until my last breath.*

And don't forget that the quickest and most effective, non-surgical face-lift you can give yourself as well as a potent way to keep your vibrational frequency in the healthy high range is to *smile*! Do it as often as you can throughout every day, when you're watching TV, driving, or doing mundane tasks. I even have a "smiley face" reminder stuck on my PC screen!

Telomeres and Breathing Technique

One more technique I use regularly is something mystics have known about and practised for centuries: deep breathing. Not only is this beneficial for one's health but scientific research has now determined that the main cause of ageing is shortening of tiny appendages to our DNA, known as *telomeres*. Using the analogy of shoelaces, think of the plastic tips at the ends that stop the laces falling apart. Similarly, telomeres are found at the tips at the end of chromosomes and stop the DNA strands from unraveling.

Furthermore, scientists have found from research with different groups of people that over time deep breathing using the abdominal muscles actually slows down the telomeres' shortening process that normally occurs as we get older. These researchers recommend daily deep breathing done slowly and consciously while paying particular attention to the end of both the in-breaths and out-breaths.

Here's where science and spirituality blend once again. Ancient wisdom teaches a technique of breathing in for eight counts, holding the breath while expanding the lungs fully for four counts; slowly exhaling for eight counts then holding the out-breath for four counts, while pushing the last vestiges of stale air out.

When I do this technique, instead of counting, I mentally say YHWH twice on the inhale, then hold for another YHWH, and then repeating the same pattern on the exhale and hold. It's a neat way of super-charging the whole process.

Placebo and Nocebo Effects

To help friends and family who are not into living from their Higher Self just yet, you can always tell them about another field of current research that's proving highly successful labeled the *placebo effect*. Orthodox people tend to rubbish the whole idea of mind over matter or the power of belief being effective. *Impossible* they say.

Not so. *The Scientific American Mind* magazine that I receive monthly continues to report about ongoing clinically-controlled experiments proving our bodies can heal themselves. If you believe something is healing you even though it turns out to be simply a sugar pill or an acted-out procedure, then it can work perfectly. And placebos often work better than conventional drugs or procedures. This is puzzling medics and pharmaceutical companies time and again. Isn't that great news? (There's a particularly powerful placebo experiment conducted by a surgeon that you can view online. The link is: **https://www.youtube.com/watch?v=HqGSeFOUsLI)**

The flip side of this positive effect, however, is what's called a *nocebo*. This is when a person is told by an authority figure like a doctor, that there's no hope or that they've only got so many weeks or months to live. In most cases, once this seed is planted in their subconscious, it sets about producing that result. In some instances, it's even shown afterwards in autopsies that a person died on cue, but not from the disease. This is similar to some aboriginal practices of "pointing the bone" or hexing someone—the effect is the same.

So should you be unfortunate enough to be told there's no cure, as I was twice, then immediately say to yourself, *I AM refusing to accept this.* Use Emergency Mind CPR and delete the seed cause to change the prognosis. This is an excellent tip to pass on to others, too.

My Favorite Anti-Ageing Mantra

In conclusion, I want to share a brilliant mantra that I use to remind myself of how I intend to live during my many more useful decades of healthy longevity, reinforcing my optimum health and wellbeing focus. It is: *I refuse to allow an old person into this body!*

And it makes me feel good, too.

CHAPTER 19
I AM Successful Fulfillment

Successful Fulfillment is the title of the fourth and final quadrant of your *Perfect Diamond of Life*. Before filling in this quadrant with specific items from your list, I suggest you do the following preparation:

Preparation

Here's your check-list to get you thinking about your subconscious programming around success and fulfillment:

- *I'm not good enough ….…*
- *I'm not as clever as ….…*
- *I've always been a born loser ….…*
- *I'm useless at ….…*
- *My sister is prettier/brother is better than me ….…*
- *I envy others their success ….…*
- *If I had more money/bigger house/better job I could be happy ….…*

How did you do with these? Most people have grown up with some kind of conditioning that has limited their life satisfaction and success. Now is the time to cancel and delete yours, as well as eradicate their seed causes.

What Is Success?

Picture this: A person is being interviewed by a TV reporter who, thrusting a microphone in their face, asks,

"Tell the viewers what is the secret of your failure?" This is unlikely to happen, of course, because all we want to know is the secret of a person's success. Success is generally regarded as the pinnacle of attainment in life which we all would love to enjoy.

But what constitutes real success? Sure, it's great to feel at the top of your game and receive accolades. If you go deeper though, you realize that the genuine feeling of success is a sense of inner fulfillment and satisfaction that is far more important than the external results. You could define success as having good self-esteem and acknowledgement of your sense of worth as a human being.

It's important to keep in mind that success is a moving target. It can change as you move towards your original goal, so don't be afraid to re-evaluate and if necessary, change the outcome you first put in place. Remember to redefine the steps or methods you originally selected accordingly, so everything stays in alignment. And it never hurts to challenge yourself to achieve more and more as you increase your manifestation mastery.

Your Success, My Success

I've enjoyed great success in multiple careers—a total of eight before my spirituality-based service career—but as I look back on those careers, they are as ephemeral as dreams. Their only lasting effects are the skills I developed and experiences that gave me greater understanding and appreciation of life. Those skills I can now bring to fulfilling what I really came here to do, my current endeavors.

For me, this means being the very best me I can be, and achieving the greatest personal spiritual progress, Self-mastery and miracle-filled life possible. It means fulfilling every facet of my ever-expanding and evolving Soul Service to others as joyfully and perfectly as I can. Real success cannot be measured in material things.

So what does success mean to you? You might like to take a moment to think about this and put it into your own words.

If you've had more challenges than most, it may be encouraging to remember this little truism: Success is falling down nine times and getting up ten times! Refuse to allow yourself to get discouraged. Small changes and improvements often come before· a dramatic change or complete outcome. Small miracles begin to occur like tastes of greater things to come. Remember to celebrate each one and notch up your progress; the small child within each one of us needs such encouragement.

Failure is Not an Option

Failure is really only a state of mind because invariably if you look at it deep enough, within every seeming failure there's a gift or learning. Developing a refusal-to-fail attitude creates the mindset to succeed and blocks out any negative thoughts from taking hold. If you find yourself heading towards labeling a setback as a failure, you could use a decree to immediately reverse the downward spiral, such as: *I refuse to allow the belief of failure into my life.*

As you work on achieving your desired outcomes, it's likely there will be times when nothing seems to be changing. Always remember that any major success is usually made up of a whole lot of small successes rather like steps along the way, and these are often a culmination of multiple attempts at overcoming certain obstacles. Small accomplishments are like building blocks to greater success.

Celebrate these little triumphs. Never allow yourself to discount their importance because they increase confidence as well as provide encouragement to keep going. Falling short of your big outcome is not failing—the only real failure would be to quit trying.

The Secret of Fulfillment

Think back to a time or occasion when you felt a deep sense of fabulous fulfillment. Apart from achieving a long-held dream, the other times were no doubt the result of helping others or engaging in a worthwhile cause or service. But you may wonder how to make this a more continual state in your life. So here's my tip:

Because my *raison d'* être is summed up by: *How may I best serve?* I regularly ask HS to bring into my conscious awareness my next most perfect step, especially when I have finished a particular project. I paraphrase the lovely way it's put in *A Course in Miracles*: *Holy Spirit, what would you have me do and when, where would you have me go and when, what would you have me say and to whom, and what would you have me write?*

These words never fail to keep me on track, making the most of every day and the rest of this incarnation. I suggest you re-word your willingness to serve in ways that fit your life. Then watch how beautiful opportunities quietly appear.

It's the Little Things that Count

Everyone, including me, gets maximum satisfaction from serving and helping other people or projects. It matters not the scale of service or whether it receives any recognition or even thanks. Simple things like helping someone in need, clearing rubbish from a public place, volunteering in an organization that supports particular groups of people or animals or the planet—all are very worthwhile and make a difference. The world needs many more volunteers behind the scenes who quietly and lovingly help make life a little better in some way.

There's another form of unspoken service, too, that often gets overlooked. Every step of progress you or I make towards fulfilling our purpose and dreams, every time we stumble but carry on anyway can serve as an inspiration to someone else. You never know who may be noticing how focused and determined you are. And you may never know how your actions may help to sustain and motivate others to hold fast to achieving their goals and dreams.

Be an example, not just set an example. Learning to live a heavenly life serves not just you but opens up the minds of people around you to the fact that they can do the same. You can share your developing knowledge of how to live far above the accepted social average to create a domino effect of more and more people able to change their lives by no longer settling for less. Imagine what a wonderful world this change in mindset and behavior can create.

The Deep Hole

Sometimes un-fulfillment manifests as a deep yearning inside, like a hole that nothing seems to fill, not even family, money, job success. You only have to read about many successful movie stars or singers who have everything on the physical level and yet are unfulfilled, often turning to drugs or alcohol to try and fill this hole. What is the only answer? I'm sure you know by now. It could be summed up as being the best expression of your Highest Self that you can be while still in human form, which also serves humanity's consciousness evolution. This unleashes your Miracle-Habit potential and is the only way to feel authentically fulfilled and complete.

What is *Heaven on Earth?*

For most people, heaven is a place or state that can only be experienced after you die, and only if you've been "good" enough. It's also associated with divine beings who live in a perfect state of bliss. So why do I and so many others hold it as a possibility for us while still on earth? People like friend and colleague Dr. Bruce Lipton who not only talked about living this blissful state at a gathering I organized, but writes about it in his latest book *The Honeymoon Effect,* which is sub-titled *The Science of Creating Heaven on Earth.*

I can only share my own perspective, but my reasoning is that the carrot of enjoying the after-life in heaven was a powerful part of religion's control strategy. It was a way of keeping people in line and making them tolerate often dreadful conditions and obey the church's doctrines without question. The threat was, and still is, held over them that if they don't measure up, then heaven isn't an option. You're doomed to eternal misery in hell.

Really? According to my dictionary, among the definitions of *heaven* are: "supreme happiness; excellent; supremely blessed; dwelling place of the gods." You can see where this is going. All these adjectives perfectly describe a state that is actually possible to live in while still on earth—if you know how. The whole purpose of my book is to share the ways I've found and tested that result in this delightful state.

I expect there's some eyebrow raising at the last meaning. But if you truly accept that we humans are embryo gods in human bodies, then earth *is* our dwelling place, at least for now. I rest my case.

What's Perfect and Heavenly For You?

We're all bound to have our own versions of a heavenly life. Maybe now is a good time to review how your ideas have gelled, seeing you've almost finished your journey through this book with me. Perhaps revisit your *Perfect Diamond of Life* and note what kind of facets would be most blissful for you, or fill in the diagram with more detail just for fun.

When I use the word *perfect* in this third dimensional sense, I'm using its generic meaning: "to do or assimilate thoroughly; a degree of excellence; highest state; fully skilled." It's obvious that in our world based upon polarities of black or white, good or bad, the higher meaning of perfect isn't possible.

However, when I use *perfect* in reference to the work and effect of my HS, then its other higher meanings of "complete" and "flawless" also apply. As you can see, I love words and aim to use them correctly.

Being Human

It's true that you can live a more heavenly and blessed life while in this dimension, but you still have feet of clay. As I explained before, you are subject to duality. While you are able to stay in your Miracle Me vibration most of the time, you are also subject to lower frequencies whether of your own and others' creation, or from the influence of mass consciousness. This is the influence of the "earth" part of the Heaven on Earth state.

Learn to be kind to yourself when you slip on your own banana skin. As the song goes, just pick yourself up, brush yourself off, start all over again, and get back on track. I remember a few years ago, I was beating myself up for not having handled a situation in the best way, saying to myself: *How on earth could you be so – so – so .....* and before I could think of the appropriate word, it popped right in: *human!*

That experience perfectly sums up what it's like to be a Miracle Me, living the Miracle Effect of I AM Mastery while still in human form. Remember, the time for miracles has not passed but is always *now*, the most glorious time of all. My deepest wish for you dear reader, is that you experience all you can possibly dream of in the coming years, living your divine potential limitlessly, joyously with comfort and ease, so the world is blessed by your inspiring presence and example.

CHAPTER 20
The Shift

You've come a long way in learning how to reclaim your miracle-filled birthright as a being of divine origin. If you have been implementing even some of the knowledge and techniques as you worked through this book, no doubt there's been more going on than you've perhaps been aware of. As well as increasing your manifestation mastery and love of life, a deep consciousness-based shift is occurring within you, even at the "baby-steps" stage.

I'm able to say this because whenever I teach the content of this book as a seminar, I notice an energetic shift happening in people, often visibly. Participants soon start looking more relaxed, happy and confident. Some of them experience amazing results just in the one day. For example, one lady who arrived in the morning, limping badly and walking with the help of a cane, came up to me at the end and was walking freely without either. When I phoned a few days later to see how she was doing, she told me that she was still walking well.

Why not take a moment and check yourself out? As it's unlikely you've been able to read and do all the techniques in one sitting, you may not experience a noticeable shift in yourself—yet. But as you integrate the knowledge and use the tools more effectively and consistently, you will begin to notice changes both inner and outer. You feel lighter in yourself, freer, more quietly content, confident and peaceful—if not all the time, at least the greater percent of the time. The fantastic news is that this Miracle Effect mindset is cumulative in its benefits and effects. And when you have the odd slip-up, remember the Divine Power of your real Self and let it go. Get back on the wagon and refocus on what you find most helpful. Before you know it, you'll be back on course. You *can* do it.

Your inner shift means that you are raising your consciousness to ever higher levels. You know your miracle-magnetizing power and reach is no longer just an aspiration or intellectual understanding; it's real, here and now. You are becoming actively miracle-conscious.

Sing a Song of Success

Here is a fun tool that succinctly summarizes the basic premise of the whole book. It is a way to encapsulate all your perfect outcomes by means of a song you can sing every day—many times each day—to keep your vibrational frequency high and embed your overall intentions in the forefront of your mind. I sing it to the tune of "Oh, What a Beautiful Morning'" from the musical *Oklahoma*. I sing it often, first thing in the morning, having a shower, when I look out on another beautiful day, when driving my car, walking my dog, and whenever I want to express my gratitude and joy for this amazing gift of life.

Enjoy! I trust it works for you as well as it does for me, helping you to *feel good—feel your God-Self.*

"My Wonderful Life"

Chorus:

> *Oh what a wonderful life I have,*
> *Perfect in every way;*
> *I've got a real certain feeling,*
> *Miracles keep coming my way.*

I've got love and wealth in great abundance,
Health and perfect ongoing fulfilment;
I'm grateful and happy for my effortless success ...
In my Diamond of Life being perfectly expressed.

Repeat Chorus – plus add at end:
Miracles keep coming my way every day,
Miracles keep coming my way – hooray!

Recap of the Four Steps

Let's recap the four essential steps you've learned to take and their ramifications, in making a quantum shift in your consciousness. These steps are the *who* you truly are, the *what* that could stop your success, the *how* to live empowered as the Divine Being you are while in physical form, and the *designed doing* of living a Heaven on Earth existence.

I've summarized the Four Steps and organized key points into a 12-point checklist that you can refer to, especially if, on occasion, life gets in the way:

1. You **know**, rather than simply believe, you can live divinely while still in physical form through the unfailing power of your I AM Higher Self that you now understand is your higher counterpart and perfect partner.
2. You communicate and work through the Holy Spirit, your interconnecting link hotline, that is always available because you have fully integrated it into your life.

3. Understanding what your Higher Self power offers you through the PEOPLISM anagram means it is now very real and usable to you every day.

4. Living and maintaining this high vibrational frequency level acts like a lightning rod, so you attract every wonderful and miraculous event, experience, situation, thing, support, outcome you can possibly imagine.

5. You know what could limit or stop your progress and how to get out of your own way. You have many tools to use to rectify any off switch blockages and get back on track, such as deleting subconscious and mental/emotional self-sabotaging programs, Mind CPR, and mindfulness.

6. Backed by your vastly increased knowledge, you have a fully equipped tool-box for the rest of your life to ensure your ultimate success.

7. Your victory is assured because you fully understand the importance of the Universal Laws of Life and implement them day by day, particularly the Laws of Acceptance, Belief/Knowing, Verification, Certainty, Commitment, Energy Exchange, Gratitude, Worthiness, Forgiveness, Oneness, Cause and Effect/Karma, Enthusiasm, Thought and Vibration.

8. You use the extraordinarily powerful techniques and concepts that restore and maintain your Divine Power flow. You keep your instrument—*you*—in tune each and every day to maximize your potential as a Miracle Me capable of magnetizing miracles.

9. Miracles both big and small become a regular part of your life because miracles are natural to aware Divine Beings like you; and you now know the four means by which they can occur: consciously,

unexpectedly, by divine orchestration or by divine intervention.

10. You are an unstoppable force for joy and good as an inspiration to others because you know and use the Perfect Outcome technique with your HS in charge to achieve success of all kinds.

11. Through understanding what makes up your personal Perfect Diamond of Life, you enjoy by decreeing and manifesting with Divine Authority all that constitutes your Heaven on Earth life. Never more do you get bogged down with concern over how or through whom your life's Perfect Diamond will manifest because your I AM HS takes care of the necessary details while you work on any Self-mastery aspects that are necessary.

12. As a manifestation master living the Miracle Effect, you are adding to the growing swell of pioneers showing a new, victorious way of living and helping to make the world a better place.

You are here because it's what you signed up for in this life: to be an agent of change. You are accomplishing this through being an inspiring example, a role model to others in the way you live your life, and sharing what works for you with others when they inquire, as no doubt they will do. By choosing to live limitlessly, you are becoming all you can be. You are making a difference in humanity's evolution of consciousness. Congratulations!

Appendix

A. My First Major Conscious Miracle

A few years ago, I was travelling from Copenhagen to Arles in France on a Friday to attend a weekend seminar starting at 10 AM the next morning. The flight was due to leave at 7:30 AM to get me into Montpellier, the nearest international airport, where after a couple of hours I'd catch the only direct train to Arles at 2 PM. It would be an easy day's travel, getting me to the small town of Arles by the afternoon, so I could settle in and be ready and rested for the seminar the next day.

After checking in for the first leg, I noticed the departure time had changed to 8 AM. No problem. But then it was changed to 11 AM. This was cutting my train link a bit close, but it was still possible by a non-direct route. But when I next checked the board expecting to see the *Boarding Now* sign, to my dismay it had been changed yet again to 7.30 PM. An announcement followed explaining that the aircraft was unfit to fly and they had to wait for some spare parts to be flown in. When I asked the airline representatives how I could get to Arles that day, as no trains or buses ran at night, they could offer no solution except to check with another airline to see if I could at least get to Paris that morning. I found all flights were full, so there was no option but to wait. Having got up at 4 AM for a 6 AM check-in at Copenhagen, it was going to be a long day.

What to do? After a brief time of feeling exasperated and concerned, I soon realized that this was another challenge I'd created to test myself on what I'd been working on and teaching for so many years. So I found a quiet place to sit where, pretending to read, I could meditate and work on creating the space and conditions for a miracle to occur.

First, I clearly defined the outcome I required, that I would be able to start the seminar effortlessly in Arles at 10 the next morning. I had absolutely no idea how this could happen, so I handed it over to my I AM Higher God-Self and its Divine Presence the Holy Spirit within. I also used the helpful affirmation for seemingly impossible situations: *God makes a way where there seems no way.* I always carry little cards I've made of some of the most powerful Divine Names in the Language of Light, so I scanned and quietly chanted them, especially the highest Name of YHWH, as I visualized my desired outcome. Continuously using Divine Name codes creates and maintains the high vibrations necessary for being in a state of miracle-consciousness.

With a relaxed attitude of certainty, trust and confidence, I consciously "let go and let God" take over—and got out of my own way to create the space for a heaven-sent miracle to occur. So often we sabotage our good intentions by trying too hard, by having doubts or tension that immediately short-circuits the process, or by trying to figure out how something can happen. Whenever I thought about the situation, I immediately returned my full focus on my cards. The psychological principle at work here is that you can only think one thought at a time. This ensures you hold only the highest one.

Arriving at the small, deserted Montpellier airport at around 10 PM, I collected my luggage and then, seeing there was no sign of the expected miracle *yet*, decided I may as well do the third dimensional thing and find the Information Desk. Surprisingly, not only was a clerk still there but he was helpful and could speak good English. When I asked him if there was any way I could get to Arles that night, he suggested a taxi. But the estimated cost, 200 Euros, approximately $400, made that out of the question.

Hmmm, hurry up eleventh-hour miracle, I thought.

The clerk then told me there might be a train connection the next morning—rather unlikely though because this route and destination are little used, especially on a weekend—and that I could stay overnight at a nearby hotel. Then a lady from the same flight, whom I hadn't noticed but just happened to be further along the desk talking to another man, said something to him. Understanding English, she had overheard our conversation and was offering to take me as far as Nimes where she lived, about an hour's journey away by car. Nimes is halfway between Montpellier and Arles, so I thought, *Well, that's at least half a miracle,* and I gladly accepted.

I must admit as I looked at her I thought, *Angels do come in surprising disguises.* An untidy middle-aged woman, she had long, lanky hair, tattered jeans, and an old sweatshirt with a couple of food stains down the front—not exactly the idealistic picture we have of angels. But an angel indeed she was, with a heart of gold.

Fortunately, Isabella's English was reasonable, and with my broken French we got along famously as we drove through the rainy night. Then quite suddenly she said, "Have you any Euros on you?" Just for a split second I thought about how here I was in a stranger's car, trusting she was going where she said she was. I immediately replaced the thought with Holy Spirit's help and said yes. I had about 40 Euros on me.

"Well," she said, "If you'd like to contribute towards the petrol, then I'll drive you right through to Arles." Even though I had been expecting a miracle, I could scarcely believe my ears, as that was another hour's drive on this miserable night – and another return journey home to Nimes for her.

With great gratitude, I happily accepted and at the petrol station took out my money ready to give Isabella most of it in return for her kindness. She sorted through it, took out one note and gave the rest back, saying that I'd need it for my trip. She had only kept five Euros—around $10. I wanted to give her more, but she wouldn't hear of it, bless her.

We arrived in Arles shortly after midnight, having no idea where the hotel was. Finding a bistro bar about to close, Isabella went in and asked how to find the hotel. Once at the location, I pressed the night button and eventually the bleary-eyed manager came down to let me in. I gratefully thanked God and Isabella who drove off into the night for yet another hour's drive home. Finally, I got to bed around 1 AM, and was at my seminar the next morning, not only on time but well rested and relaxed.

To me this was a true miracle. Not in my wildest imagination could I have come up with the incredible sequence of events, especially the unexpected, generous help from a complete stranger. My outcome was so effortlessly and perfectly fulfilled. Yes, miracles *do* happen—and you can learn how to allow the miracle-working Divine Power latent within you to bring them into form.

B. Laws of the Mind: The Art of Mind Power and Control Through the 9 Laws of Thought

Your thoughts are the tools of your mind, and in turn your brain is the tool you use to generate your thoughts. Therefore, you have absolute control over your thoughts. To effect any change in your life, you first need to know how the mind works through understanding and then aligning with these Laws of the Mind.

This science of the mind reveals the third-dimensional secret of self-mastery and manifestation or creation. You and I live in a world we create with our thoughts due to the fact that all thoughts carry the potential for creating form. Ultimately the goal is to become completely conscious of every sustained thought you have. Only then can you become master of your personal world and your life.

These Laws of the Mind are among the most important principles you need to understand and apply for positive and fulfilling daily living, as well as for achieving your long-term goals. Your thoughts of today create your tomorrows.

Until you know how your thinking processes work and then put these laws into moment by moment practice, so much of your potential will be unrealized, and you will not achieve your heart's desires. Otherwise, it's like having the most amazingly complex bio-computer ever created for your own personal use, but without an instruction manual.

So what are these all-important and powerful laws, or the mind's "instructions for use," and how do they work?

1. *Thoughts become things.* Thought is real energy, and energy is never lost, only transformed. The power of thought can become a physical creation, especially when a thought is focussed on for any

length of time. (It will manifest in the physical more quickly and perfectly when you follow the Master Gardener's guidelines in #5 below.) This occurs because of the truth of the next three laws.

2. *Where your attention or focus goes, there the creative energy flows.* We've all proved this law at some time or another when we've wanted something so much that it's all we thought about until it appeared.

3. *You are the only person who can think in your mind.* You are the Managing Director of your mind and thoughts. Only you can hire or fire the thoughts you choose to select and think. Contrary to popular belief, no-one else can *make* you think in certain ways—unless you allow it.

4. *Whatever you believe becomes true for you.* Just observe how what anyone really believes eventually becomes a reality, which in turn confirms for them that their belief is right! And if you look honestly at yourself, you'll see the same applies. I've been finding that it's well worth examining the beliefs I hold, so that I can see if they're serving me or not.

You may recall how programs or patterns you picked up from other people, particularly as a child, are held in your subconsciousness and run your life whether you're aware of them or not. Whatever your subconscious mind believes as fact will play out in your life. And remember the quickest way to release negative thoughts and beliefs that disempower you is to use the Emergency Mind CPR technique in

Chapter 13. You may have to do this repeatedly, until you know they're cancelled and you don't feel any energy or emotional charge around them when you check them.

5. *Every thing you do starts with a single thought.* Think of each single thought you want to create or manifest as a seed thought. Picture your subconscious mind as an inner garden with rich and fertile soil, so that anything you plant in it will flourish and produce an abundant harvest. Your life accurately reflects the condition of your inner garden and the sorts of seed thoughts you've planted, whether positive or negative—you won't get carrots if you plant dandelion seeds. It's useful perhaps to see yourself as the Master Gardener and how an analogy of the inner garden of your mind works, including fertilising your implanted seeds with enthusiasm, certainty and anticipation, daily weeding out any negative thoughts, scepticism or doubts.

Lastly, bear in mind that plants don't grow overnight. It takes some time for the seeds to germinate, then grow, and eventually produce their harvest. The same applies to manifesting your goals.

6. *You can only think one thought at a time.* We think around 50,000 thoughts a day, leading many to be under the mistaken impression that we have several thoughts in our mind at once. That is not so. Even though your thoughts flow through your mind at lightning speed, you actually can only think one

thought at a time. Think of how a movie is made up of countless frames running at such enormous speed that they give the impression of continuous movement.

7. *Thoughts behave like boomerangs.* They always return because they stay connected to their source, maybe not straight away but return they will. And because of the Law of Attraction and Energy, thoughts that are weighted or charged with emotion act like magnets and attract similar thoughts. Emotions have "weight" and power, so they send out strong signals that link them with similar energies, making them "loaded" or "charged." This means that they multiply often hundreds of times over by the time you receive them back.

Think of some colloquial sayings: a situation is "charged with emotion," you get a sense of a "heavy" atmosphere. Or notice how one negative person will soon attract others who add to the original emotion or agree with the statement. So before you charge it, change it.

8. *Your mind is both a sending and a receiving station of thought.* And so is everyone else's. Your mind is like a two-way radio with no off switch. It's "on the air" 24 hours a day, 365 days a year, transmitting and receiving all the time. You are always affecting others and your environment with your thoughts, and if you allow it, other people's thoughts are affecting you.

9. *Your inner and outer worlds are connected by thought.* You actually live in both worlds simultaneously. They are independent of each other and yet connected. The *outer world* consists of situations, experiences—what most call reality—our external world of the body, things, and circumstances. Your *inner world* that you live in at the same time consists of your feelings, thoughts, sensations, emotions and memories.

For example, what did you have for breakfast this morning? Where were you this time last week? You're still sitting reading this, and yet in your inner world you had briefly left and popped back to this morning or last week in order to remember. So you are living in both worlds simultaneously, although many think they are one and the same. Unfortunately, until you become aware of this fact, you mirror inside whatever happens in your outer world by taking it into your mind and emotions. Things happen outside of you, and you react in your inner world. And equally important is the fact that your outer world also mirrors your inner world.

Sadly, most tend to use this incredible instrument of the mind mainly as a reactor, and yet it is the greatest creative energy generator ever made. It actually is creating our outer reality all the time. What you're thinking will, if your attention is held onto it, become a physical reality or thing. The secret is to use your mind as a generator rather than merely a reactor; otherwise you are wasting the incredible mind power you have at your disposal. In each moment the choice is yours.

C. The God Code in Your DNA

My comprehension of God comes from the deeply felt conviction of a superior intelligence that reveals itself in the knowable world.

Albert Einstein

Modern science defines the basic elements of creation that make up our physical world and our physical bodies by numbers and letters. The four bases of DNA are an abbreviation for groupings of the four elements represented by the letters A, T, C, and G. While the same elements of hydrogen, nitrogen, oxygen and carbon are present in each DNA base, it is the amount of each element that varies. So rather than having to write out how many times the actual element occurs each time the base is noted, they are simply implied by the appropriate letter.

By taking one of the 17 key characteristics or properties that are described by number from the Periodic Table of Elements, that of atomic mass, and following the principles of Gematria that allow us to simplify numbers to one digit, we find its simple mass number. Gematria is a numerological study that shows that words or phrases adding to the same number total are in some way related. This occurs by revealing the hidden relationships and deeper layers of meaning that would normally be overlooked by simply reading the words or phrases themselves. According to how we define any science today, the study of Gematria can be considered an ancient science as it yields precise and repeatable outcomes from specific operations between letters, phrases and words.

To return to the simple mass numbers of the main elements that make up our physical world and bodies: hydrogen is represented by the number 1, nitrogen by 5, and oxygen by 6. Not only do these equate to ancient references to the alchemical elements of creation, Fire, Air and Water, but by numerical correspondence, they also relate to the letter symbols that form the name of God in our earliest sacred languages. For example, one of these letter symbols alphabet derived from the original Language of Light, used continuously for over 3000 years, is *Hiburu*, or ancient Hebrew-Aramaic.

The Hebrew letters of the Name of God, *YHWH*, exactly equate numerically to the simple mass of hydrogen, nitrogen and oxygen. Similarly, the same letters in Arabic do the same. The fourth element that makes up our DNA bases, carbon, is by correspondence the letter relating to earth and our physicality. The chances of these correspondences occurring randomly is .00042 percent!

This amazing insight has been thoroughly researched, and two books I can personally recommend on the topic are *The Book of Knowledge: the Keys of Enoch* by Dr J.J. Hurtak, who approaches the whole subject from a scientific and genetic viewpoint in Key 202; and *The God Code* by Gregg Braden.

In *The God Code*, Gregg, author of many books including *Awakening to Zero Point* and *The Isaiah Effect*, explains this correspondence by saying that there is a mathematical and numerical link between ancient sacred alphabets (like Hebrew), the letters of those alphabets, and the DNA of the cells of our body. He points out that through that link, when we look at the chemical codes within our body, the numbers make it possible for us to replace the chemicals with the letters because they match. The DNA begins to spell words, and the words begin to spell sentences. Our genetic code spells the ancient Name of God transliterated as YHWH. The same name lives within all humans, regardless of any differences, whether real or perceived. This inner relationship between all mankind was described in sacred texts, such as the Hebrew *Sepher Yetzirah* at least 3000 years before modern science verified such connections.

D. My Personal Daily Decrees

These are representative of how I word my decrees, but as I've advised, they are not fixed and can be varied at will to keep them fresh and alive. Especially note that creating your own wording often makes the decree more powerful and meaningful to you.

Daily Gratitude Decree

I AM so happy and grateful for my Beloved I AM's Power and Substance filling my consciousness, mind and body, so that all the miraculous aspects of my Perfect Diamond of Life are manifesting perfectly now and always:

- *Abundance of Love to give and receive from family, friends, acquaintances, colleagues, neighbors, and all who bless and enrich my life past, present and future.*
- *Perfect pain-free health and functioning of my beautiful body that serves me so well with abundant energy, vitality, permanent rejuvenation, agelessness, and youthfulness throughout my many decades of healthy longevity.*
- *Abundant fulfillment and success in all I do now and always, both personally and as my Soul Service.*
- *Abundance of beauty, peace, tranquility, within me and in my home sanctuary, and ongoing flow of money into my accounts to live with comfort and ease.*

It is so.

Short version of Daily Gratitude Decree

I'm so happy and grateful for the love that fills my life; for all those who bless and enrich my life past, present and future; for my wonderful body that serves me so well in optimum health and function; for satisfying success and fulfillment in all I do; and for abundance of all things that help make my life heaven on earth.

Meditation Conclusion Decree:

By the fully active Invincible Power of my I AM, I decree that this day and every day, my personal life and affairs through the manifestation of my perfect Diamond of Life so I enjoy Heaven on Earth; my spiritual progress, Self-Mastery and manifestation-mastery to the highest possible levels—and miracles; and every facet of my expanding Soul Service—unfolds joyfully, effortlessly, and perfectly with comfort and ease.

So it is.

Forgiveness Decree

Dear brothers and sisters everywhere who may have suffered from my ignorant, unloving thoughts, words or deeds in this or any lifetime, please forgive me for my temporary limitations. I AM deeply sorry to have caused you pain.

I also forgive you from my heart for all your ignorant, unloving words and actions from which I suffered in this or any lifetime. Today I gladly release all grudges or feelings of resentment I may have held against you or myself.

I seek no revenge or retaliation, nor do I project guilt upon you. I release you, and as I forgive myself I AM released. You are free and so am I.

We are One Self united in our Creator. Such is the Truth that sets us free.

E. Your Perfect Diamond of Life

What do YOU most desire – and require?

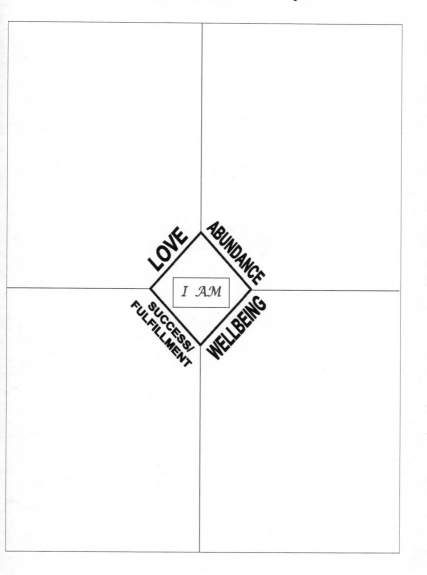

Bibliography

1. Achad, Frater, *Melchizedek Truth Principles* (Great Seal Press, USA, 1963)
2. Achad, Frater, *Ancient Mystical White Brotherhood* (Great Seal Press, USA, 1971)
3. *A Course in Miracles* (Foundation for Inner Peace, California, USA, 1975)
4. Braden, Gregg, *The God Code* (Hay House, USA, 2004)
5. Chase, Dr Paul Foster, *Builders of the Adytum Home Study Mystery School* (Los Angeles, USA, 1961)
6. Chopra, Dr. Deepak, *The Seven Spiritual Laws of Success* (Amber-Allen Publishing, USA, 1994)
7. Clark, Glenn, *The Man Who Tapped the Secrets of the Universe* (University of Science and Philosophy, USA, 1946)
8. Hall, Manly P, *The Secret Teachings of all the Ages* (The Philosophical Research Society Inc, 1901)
9. Hay, Louise, *You Can Heal Your Life* (Hay House, USA, 1984)
10. Hurtak, Dr. James J, *The Book of Knowledge: The Keys of Enoch* (The Academy for Future Science, USA, 1977)
11. Lipton, Bruce, *The Biology of Belief* (Mountain of Love, USA, 2005)
12. Lipton, Bruce, *The Honeymoon Effect* (Hay House, USA, 2013)
13. McTaggart, Lynne, *The Field* (Harper Collins, London, 2001)

14. Pistis Sophia *Coptic Gnostic Scrolls Translation from the Nag Hammadi Library* (The Academy for Future Science, USA, 1999; commentary by Drs. J. J. and D Hurtak)
15. *Scientific American Mind*, magazines published monthly (Scientific American Inc, NY, USA)
16. Shinn, Florence Scovel, *The Game of Life and How to Play It* (Fowler Ltd, London, 1925)
17. *Three Initiates,* The Kybalion (1908; Dover Edition, USA, 2009)

Acknowledgements

I am deeply indebted to the long line of mystics, initiates, and masters that stretches back many centuries, and to those who through their own personal divine connection brought through spiritual truths and principles that they left for posterity—for us today. These revelations and deep understandings form the vast body of priceless knowledge known as Ancient Wisdom. That Ancient Wisdom is just as relevant today, even though we may couch it in our modern terms and idioms, and explain its veracity through today's sciences.

I am grateful for all the more recent mystics and authors whose insights expand upon the ageless teachings and inspire us to work on our evolution of consciousness towards becoming a perfect expression of our divinity while still in human form.

But most of all, I honor my own personal divine connection, my I AM Higher Self who gives me ongoing understandings, revelations and inspiration through my Divine Presence within, the Holy Spirit. This stupendous gift each one of us has at our disposal fills me with awe and deep gratitude.

My deepest appreciation goes to the many "angels in disguise," people whose loving support blesses and enriches both my personal life and my service work. In particular, Alistair Hutchison who, as one of my earliest graduates in the 1990s, has generously supported my expanding Soul Service and many projects ever since, including this book—I can never thank him enough. I am most grateful to Jeltje Kooistra who is my uncomplaining webmaster and "sounding board" as well as dear friend. And to Leighton Durney who so willingly and competently handles all the necessary technical and IT aspects of my work.

My thanks to all of the thousands of students and attendees of my local and international seminars, lectures and events over the years, and especially to the many graduates of my *OM* International Mystery School trainings who repeatedly asked if I'd written a book. I used to answer *no* because teaching is my role, but they have continued to encourage me to write down some of what I live and teach, so more people worldwide can benefit. Well, here it is! Your continued support is deeply appreciated, and yes, there are more books to come in this *I AM Mastery* series! Thanks, too, to Leigh Cain and Sue Law who carefully went through my manuscript and gave valuable feedback.

And my thanks to Nancy Marriott, the perfect editor, whose skill, expertise and understanding has guided me so my teachings have been transformed into a readable book that's clear and accessible to all.

May the love, support and generosity of all these Divine people be returned to them, blessed and multiplied.

About the Author

Sylvia Vowless QSM (Queen's Service Medal for community service)

For the past 30 years, Sylvia Vowless has dedicated her life to serve. As an internationally recognized authority on the Western Ancient Wisdom tradition, she is also known as an expert spiritual master teacher, visionary, and professional inspirational speaker. She is a published writer in numerous spiritual publications worldwide, and her books so far include *Soul Education*, a *Metaphysical A—Z Dictionary*; *The Universal Laws*, and a year-long *Home Study Online Series* which is used by serious students from more than a dozen countries around the world as their spiritual foundation.

Since the 1990s, she has been a guest presenter at more than 30 spiritual international conferences in countries as diverse as Brazil, Denmark, Germany, Austria, the UK, Australasia, and the US. She was chosen in 2005 to be the Spiritual Ambassador for the southern hemisphere, and flown to Istanbul, Turkey to present a paper at the *Call to World Peace and Unity* Symposium. In 1996, she was asked to establish the Melchizedek Academy of Soul Education International which continues to serve through the *OM* International Modern Mystery School for the 21st Century. Incorporating today's scientific insights with ageless wisdom, its aim is to help empower people to reach their highest spiritual and human potential.

Sylvia's passion since the 1960s has been the study, research, application and verifying of the Western mystical lineage of Ancient Wisdom principles and Universal Laws. Her studies have included the pre-Judaic Universal Tree of Life, Western Qaballah, Gnosticism, and the Pistis Sophia scrolls from the Nag Hammadi library that record the resurrected Jesus' advanced teachings to His disciples. Modern sacred texts she has spent years studying include *A Course in Miracles, The Book of Knowledge: the Keys of Enoch*, and the *Pistis Sophia*. She uses her Godself-given gift of distilling such ageless knowledge in order to share it clearly and usefully with others, combining it with her own ongoing Higher Self revelations and understandings.

Originally trained as a school and ballet teacher, Sylvia has had eight previous careers that have included being the New Zealand PR/public speaker/travel advisor for the international Qantas Airline; a spiritual numerologist, counsellor and mentor; and an ethnic dance company founder/director/choreographer. All have given her skills and experience that she now uses in her "real career" and service of helping as many people as possible to transform their lives.

Sylvia was inspired to establish *ICHEC—International Collaboration for Humanity's Evolution of Consciousness—* under which she organizes regular conferences, gatherings and speaking/teaching tours for leading-edge international teachers/writers visiting New Zealand. In 2014, her New Consciousness Conference was privileged to have Dr. J J Hurtak and Dr. Desiree Hurtak as Keynote speakers. In 2015, her One Light Gathering in February was blessed with Dr. Bruce Lipton as Keynote speaker.

Her burning desire is to serve, a mission that the late Dr. Wayne Dyer captured perfectly in his words: "Any burning desire is placed there not by your personality but by your Higher Self, and it is there because the Universal Divine Mind wants it to be there. Not only that, it is your destiny to fulfil it before you die because it is your one true purpose for being here in the first place."